WE RANT AND WE ROAR

WE RANT
AND WE ROAR

THE LATEST COLLECTION OF
NEWFOUNDLAND HUMOUR BY

AL CLOUSTON

WITH A FOREWORD BY
ART SCAMMELL

Manufactured in Canada by Webcom Limited

ISBN 0-9690904-1-2
WE RANT AND WE ROAR
PUBLISHED 1980 BY
AL CLOUSTON
P.O. BOX 5922
ST. JOHNS, NEWFOUNDLAND
A1C 5X4

DEDICATION

As when we were reviewing the same subject two years ago, we must now be true for a second time, to the people who moulded this island's love of fun.

So we say the same as we said before. This book is dedicated to all humourous characters of Newfoundland, past and present, who without knowing it made life bearable. They did this through their unconscious production of fun which is good for both body and soul.

Who said it is not always known, but how better can we remember them than to record and pass on their contributions for generations, present and future, to enjoy.

Squid-jiggin' Ground

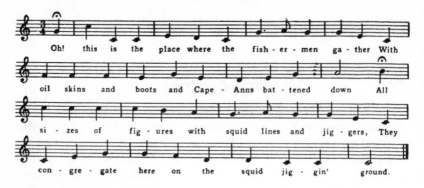

Oh! this is the place where the fish-er-men ga-ther With
oil skins and boots and Cape-Anns bat-tened down All
si-zes of fig-ures with squid lines and jig-gers, They
con-gre-gate here on the squid jig-gin' ground.

Some are workin' their jiggers while others are
yarnin',
There's some standin' up and some more
lyin' down,
While all kinds of fun, jokes and tricks are
begun
As they wait for the squid on the squid-jiggin'
ground.

There's men from the Harbour and men from
the Tickle,
In all kinds of motor boats, green, gray and
brown;
There's a red-headed Tory out here in a dory.
A runnin' down Squires on the squid-jiggin'
ground.

There's men of all ages and boys in the bargain,
There's old Billy Chafe and there's young
Raymond Brown;
Right yonder is "Bobby" and with him is
"Nobby",
They're a-chawin' hard tack on the squid-
jiggin' ground.

There's poor Uncle Billy, his whiskers are
spattered
With spots of the squid juice that's flyin'
around.
One poor little boy got it right in the eye
But they don't care a hang on the squid-
jiggin' ground.

The man with the whiskers is old Jacob Steele;
He's gettin' well up but he's still pretty sound;
While Uncle Bob Hawkins wears three pairs
of stockin's
Whenever he's out on the squid-jiggin'
ground.

God bless my sou'wester there's Skipper
John Chaffey.
He's the best man at squid-jiggin' here,
I'll be bound.
Hello! What's the row? Why, he's jiggin'
one now—
The very first squid on the squid-jiggin'
ground.

Holy smoke! What a bussel; all hands are
excited.
It's a wonder to me that nobody is drowned.
There's a bussel, confusion, a wonderful
hussel;
They're all jiggin' squid on the squid-
jigging ground.

Says Bobby: "The squid are on top of the
water
I just got me jigger about one fathom down"—
When a squid in the boat squirted right down
his throat
And he's swearin' like mad on the squid-
Jiggin' ground.

Now if you ever feel inclined to go squiddin'
Leave your white shirt and collars behind in the town,
And if you get cranky without a silk hanky
You'd better steer clear of the squid-jiggin' ground.
—*A. R. Scammel.*

FOREWORD

All peoples possess the gift of humour in greater or less degree. Radio and T.V. comedians make a living out of it with the help of gag writers and expensive props. Newfoundlanders have always created their own humour, sharing it generously and accepting it in the same spirit.

That is why most of us can afford to shrug off the pitiful attempts of outsiders who try to sharpen their dull wits at our expense with "Newfie jokes." Like the Newfoundland dog which shows his disdain for the snapping crackie at his heels with a bored yawn.

The Good Book says, "To everything there is a season, a time to laugh and a time to cry." And Newfoundlanders would rather laugh than cry. It's better for the digestion and easier on the folks around us. We've proved it over the centuries.

Most of us have our own private store of original humourous stories garnered from childhood memories or adult observation. When we foregather in groups we trot them out, each trying to top the last storyteller's bid for attention. Even before the last grin or belly laugh dies away we know our best story will be bettered by somebody else in the group. That is how it should be. May it always be so!

Al Clouston has applied his considerable talents to collecting and passing on original Newfoundland stories and incidents in print and on recordings. His touches of dialect and accent lend authenticity especially to critical Newfoundland ears.

Even as you read this, youngsters and oldsters from Ha Ha Bay to Breakheart Point, from St. Shotts in the south to Nain in Labrador, are lightening the daily round with humour that will never see print or tape. But Al Clouston has saved some of it. Enjoy.

Art Scammell

'TIS THIS WAY

How much we need fun and laughter in our lives! Somehow, some of us do not associate having fun as being Christian, but listen to a quote from President Eisenhower. To a class of undergraduates he said, "I mean it, the day that goes by without your having fun—the day you do not enjoy life—is not only unnecessary but unchristian.

If we read the contents of this book keeping in mind that the people who said all this were having fun, we will realize that folklore humour is just that, puting people over a barrel without hurting them.

If we are looking at a documentary, listening to or reading about a fact of life, then I think the subject takes on more significance for us. When I give a talk on Newfoundlandia I ask my listeners to use their imagination and try and see the people whom I describe in a story. If they do this then what I say becomes the words of these characters.

Since publishing this humour it naturally followed that I have become known and easily recognized. People walk towards me and although I have never met them they will smile and stop and want to talk. My friends approach me and we are laughing before we start talking. I told this in public one night and one person in the audience spoke up and said, "You must be retarded!" My reply was, "If that is being retarded I hope I never get all my marbles back". What a grand relationship to have with people, for them to want to stop and chat and have a laugh with you!

In my writing I have often referred to Newfoundland folklore humour as belonging to the outport people, and how indebted we should be, because without them there would be no outports and no outport humour.

In no other province are the rural communities referred to as "outports". I have been asked why they have been called outports. The word has definitely been borrowed from the British Isles. Its application in Newfoundland ties in exactly. If we look up the word in Webster's we will find—"Outport,—In Great

Britian, a port some distance from the seat of trade, especially any port but London". Quoting from the Oxford dictionary, "Outport—London was the chief port in customs collection and all other ports where customs were collected were called outports". This means that Liverpool and many other seaports were outports. For my money it was a perfectly good word brought here by our forefathers, and what's wrong with it?

We have just mentioned Great Britian and since Newfoundland was eventually settled by the English and Irish, it is only natural to find much of their vervacular still alive through out the Island.

I remember in 1929 spending a year at the old Memorial College now the Memorial University of Newfoundland. We had a physics professor fresh from England whose vernacular was almost devoid of R's. A large wooden packing case had arrived containing new equipment for the lab. Mr. Harling, our professor, seeing the caretaker, Mr. Sandy Cook, go by the door, raised his voice and said, "Oi say Sandy, do you 'ave erra ommah eah?" Sandy said, "we had one, but we killed it Christmas time". Then whispering to me he asked what did Mr. Harling ask for. I told him to get the man a hammer. From that time on Harling was known to all the boys as "ommah".

So don't blame us if we sound a little strange to you. We get our h'accent from H'England and H'Ireland. And now, listen to our fun and accents.

Al Clouston

ACKNOWLEDGEMENTS

One may have considerable knowledge about a subject but to present an acceptable product, he may have to call on others to listen to what at times may become tiring. It becomes tiring because they are asked to be judge and jury in order to select the best of several versions of the same product.

My wife Mary did not tire and to her I am grateful.

In my opinion a book of humour has to have action. Derm Duggan once more demonstrates how to use the power of drawings to complement the power of words.

My thanks goes to Derm.

INTRODUCTION

It is not impossible that the 'Newfie Joke' has lost much of its momentum due to the fact that,—who laughs at their newly rich relatives? Oil or no oil our island people will continue to create the humour that has become our heritage.

The book of Proverbs, 17:22 reads, "Being cheerful keeps you healthy. It is slow death to be gloomy". As I go about our island meeting the people it is evident that a great percentage of them have read their Bible for they are not gloomy people. A couple of years ago I remember listening to Don Harron on his C.B.C. program "Morning Side", and he remarked that travelling about Newfoundland nearly everyone you meet wants to tell you a funny story. It will take many moons to change us.

Demand for our humour in print has been demonstrated by the acceptance of a book titled, "Come 'Ere Till I Tells Ya". This is a book published in 1978. It has reached into many corners of Canada. It has also reached sales proportions to the point of four printings and was a Canadian best seller after its first printing.

"WE RANT AND WE ROAR", is more of the same. More of what is created exclusively by fellas from "over 'ome", meaning our outports. One has to be alert and sharp of wit to say the things they do without a moments hesitation.

I hasten to add once more that I don't take credit for any of it. My talent is only in the retelling of it and then publishing our folklore humour for all to enjoy.

Al Clouston

PRIEST AND BEER BOTTLES

Visiting Bonavista for a few days in October 1979, my wife and I were entertained by a visitor who came one evening to the house where we were staying. He told us stories about happenings of thirty or forty years ago, which took place where he lived. The following is such a story.

The Roman Catholic priest of that area had to attend a meeting in St. John's for four or five days. The regular caretaker was indisposed and the priest employed a nineteen year old young fellow to see to things while he was away.

On the third day of the priest's absence, the young chap wandered down to the basement of the rectory and noticed, amongst other things, about twenty cases of empties. The next day he thought he would examine the contents of the cases. During this operation the priest returned unexpectedly and surprised the young caretaker.

AND WHAT ARE YOU UP TO MIKE?

BEER BEER BEER BR BEER

OH FATHER, FATHER!! WELL FATHER I WAS T'IRSTY AN' I TAUT I WOULD HAVE A LOOK AN' SEE IF DERE WAS ONE BOTTLE DERE WITHOUT D'CAP OFF.

MIKE YOU NEED NOT WORRY ABOUT THEM, FOR THEY ARE ALL DEAD MEN IN THOSE CASES

BEER BEER

YES FATHER, AN I DON'T TINK YOU NEED TO WORRY IDER - CUZ I KNOW DEY ALL SAW D'PRIEST BEFORE DEY DIED

1

DERE'S NUTIN' WRONG WID DAT B'Y

In every community a certain percentage of the population believe that the government is fair game and if they can fulfil their needs by getting any government department to pay for them, then, "Dere's nutin' wrong wid dat b'y!" It is like an incurable disease and lasts all through their lives.

I live on Forest Road, and a quarter of a mile further down Forest Road, there are three government institutions, the General Hospital, Fever Hospital and Her Majesty's Penitentiary. It was one day in May, 1960, that I had a humourous encounter on Forest Road with one of those curious people who will get the government to pay for anything they can.

My mother had died the day before and I was on my way to our old home and this encounter gave me the laughs I needed.

While proceeding to my car, a man shouted to me from across the road. I looked over and saw a man who was about fifty-five years of age, he was using a cane and was obviously quite crippled. I walked over to him and as I approached, he said without any preliminaries, "Skipper, Skipper, where do you get d'passes? I want a pass to get in d' 'ospital." (In those days a pass was a written order from the Department of Health to admit one to the Hospital). I replied that he would have to see Mr. Harding. "Yes," he said, "I minds 'n now, dat's 'e's name, 'Ardin'. Ol man, where do I find 'ee?" I told him he would have to go to the Confederation Building. "Confederation Buildin', wat's dat ol' man?" "That's Joey's new home," I replied. "Yes," he said, "I 'erd 'e 'ad a new 'OME. Dat's it is it? 'Ow do I get in dere?" So I said "get in with me, I'll give you a race in." And in surprise he said, "will eh?"

We proceeded to my car and drove to the Confederation Building. As we did so, a one sided conversation ensued.

My friend started this way, "Just down to see d'missus, they're gonna give 'er a release d' fifteen of d' mont' an' I'm gonin' carry 'er 'ome to   . She's down in d'Penitentiary." (she was there for bootlegging.) That gave me the first laugh because I thought he was going to say the hospital. He continued "I was some h'ugly wid dem down dere dis marnin' b'y. Dey only allowed me ten minutes to look at 'er through d' bars. She got some fat d' winter b'y. Young see, b'y." I said, "How old is she"? "Farty-eight", he said. Than he went on and here is where the government is fair game, "I wants a pass now to go in the 'ospital so I won't have to pay any board while I'm waitin' fer d'missus, see 'ol man."

The conversation continued much the same as this until we arrived at the Confederation Building. As he got ready to get out of the car, he turned to me and asked, "How much is dis gonna cost to carry me in 'ere 'ol man?" I told him nothing and he turned to me quickly and announced loudly "OOOH, YOU WERKS FER D'GOVAMENT".

A GOOD USE FOR STICKIN' PLASTER

In December of 1975 I was in Grand Falls. The Colonial Broadcasting Company arranged for me to be on their open line. For most of two hours I was telling stories and talking to people who called in to tell me some humourous happenings. It was a grand morning of laughter.

Near the end of the programme a lady phoned in and asked, "Dis you H'Uncle Al?" to which I replied, "I allow maid". Then she said, "'ave dey got any stickin' plaster up dere in dat radio station?" I said, "I don't know". Then she said, "If dey 'avn't got any you tell en to sen' out and git it, an' stick it on your end, an' stick ya to d'chair, so we can 'ave a laugh all day."

BACK FROM THE MOON

Much of our Newfoundland humour, I call circumstantial humour. The circumstances exist and some witty fellow brings out the humour. We all remember Skylab and all the news about it early in 1979. Skylab was down and most people had forgotten about it when the following took place.

Some of the most sharp witted people come from the Southern Shore and the nurse who made this remark, belongs to that area of Newfoundland.

In one of the clinics at the Janeway Hospital, just after Skylab had come to earth, a doctor, who was not in too good a mood, was asked by the nurse where was he going for his holidays.

THE FLYING CAT.

Walking along the lobby of the Gander Airport some years ago, I met an old school friend of mine, Eric Winsor, the airport manager. We were quite pleased to see one another and he invited me to his home for dinner.

After dinner Roland Goodyear and Tom Dalton along with their wives came to visit. You can say we had a night of laughter. Each one took his turn at telling stories until two o'clock in the morning.

There is one memorable story that Roland Goodyear told which I think is a very funny yarn. It is a story about his hunting days and the guide who acted as guide and cook.

He told that it was customary to wait until Mac, the guide, had all his chores done, and then invite him to have a few drinks. After Mac had had four or five drinks, then in addition to being guide and cook, he became their entertainment. Mac was a great fabricator and actually made up his stories as he went along.

One particular night he started to tell about his family. He got to the subject of age and then went on as follows:

"Me family lived to a wudaful h'age. Me mudder lived to be h'eighty an'den she died in chile birt'. An' me fauder, ee lived to be ninety, ee died of nuttin' serious dough, ee just up an' perished. Of course me sister died when she waz h'eighteen but dat wazn't 'er fault dat waz d' pills d' doctor gauve'er.

Now we 'ad a cat 'ome an' me fauder 'ated en. Now d' cat knowed fauder 'ated en, an we 'ad a flagpole 'ome mose a 'undred feet 'igh, an when me fauder would come in d' 'ouse, d' cat would go out d' door or out d' windy, an' ee wouldn't stop till ee got to d' top of en.

One spring dat pole blowed down, dere waz nar foot of en leaved. Me fauder came 'ome a week after dat, an' d' cat went out d' door, an' e waz farty feet in d' air before ee knowed d'pole was blowed down.

After dat me fauder said to do 'way wid en fer sure. So I took en out to d'choppin' block an' chopped d'ead of en. T'rew d' cat one way an' d'ead d'udder. We waz sat down 'avin 'a cup a tea at midnight an' we 'eard a scratchin' at d'windy, we'auled back d' curtain, an what do ya t'ink—dere waz dat damm cat wid ee's 'ead in ee's mout'.

5

BADGER'S QUAY

About two months ago I had a very pleasant surprise when I received a phone call from Art Wicks. Art is often on the C.B.C. Fisherman's Broadcast at 5:30. He always has something worthwhile to contribute and to me he's delightful to listen to.

He talked over a small piece of business with me and then he finished by saying, "Al b'y, we had all the fish plants on strike back in January and I met an old fella who said, "H'Art b'y, you knows all dem fellers what bees on strike, dey trows down d'knife and cuffs an' won't listen to nobody. Well H'Art b'y, I t'inks dem fellers are gettin' mose of dere h'exercise, be Jumpin' to conclusions."

MAN WENT TO THE MOON? NEVER!

Visiting Stephenville last winter a clergyman told me about an old gentleman in Grey River who was arguing with some younger fellows.

The subject for argument, "Did a man go to the moon?" Believe it or not many older people would not or could not take it aboard, that a man ever got to the moon.

On the wharf in Gray River the old gentleman told the younger fellows, "No, no zar. No zar. No man ever got on the moon. No zar. D'Lard wouldn't let en git on d'moon. No".

The discussion went on and eventually the old man thought he would give in a little and in his humour he said, "Tell youse fellers what I'll do. I allow ee didn't git on en when ee wuz in d'firse quarter, but ee might a got on en when ee wuz vull, a vull moon".

DERM DUGGAN

SURELY A SCOTSMAN

Early in 1979 a Scotsman came to St. John's harbour with his small boat. His intention was to row across the Atlantic to Scotland. He left St. John's and many well wishers were on hand to see him off.

A number of reports came to St. John's with reference to his progress, and they were published in the local press.

I was in Catalina talking to the Lions Senior Citizens party! The chairman Bob Lane said that he had been talking to his bother and mentioned how well the Scotsman was doing rowing across the Atlantic. His brother's reply was, "Yes, bloody Scotsman, he'd be doin' much better if he hadn't been so tight and put an outboard motor on 'er.

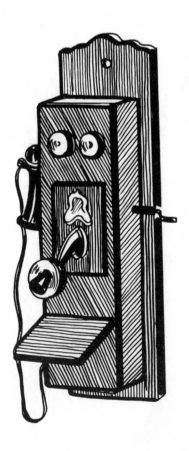

NO PLACE TO GO

A mourner arrived at the mortuary rooms to visit the family of his deceased friend. He approached the open casket and stood silently for a few moments, contemplating his relationship with the deceased. Several times a subdued laugh came from him.

One of the other visitors came over to him and asked for an explanation.

THE CORRECT ANSWER

Last year I had a news paper boy twelve years of age. One Saturday morning he appeared with a little fellow six years old.

Al: Is this your brother?

Newsboy: Yes sir.

Al: Any more home like him?

Newsboy: Yes, three other brudders.

Al: Any sisters?

Newsboy: Yes, two sir.

Al: That's makes seven of you.

Six year old: Dere's nine of us, mudder and fauder too.

Al: Who does all the cooking?

Six year old: Oi gets me own breakfast.

Al: Do you cook it or pour it out of a carton?

Six year old: Oi eats it!

THE CANDLE HELPED

A young Roman Catholic couple were quite disappointed that after five years of married life, no offspring was in sight. On one occassion when their priest visited, they discussed the subject with him. He suggested that they put up a light as a remedy for the situation. They advised him that they had done so on several occassions but without success.

On the priest's next visit he said that he had been chosen to make a visit to Rome and while there he would light a candle in Rome for them and probably that would start things happening.

On his return to Newfoundland he was transferred to another parish and did not see the childless couple for about four years. When he did visit them, however, he discovered that they now had five children, two sets of twins and one single. He remarked to the wife "My, my, the candle in Rome worked? Where is your husband?" The reply, "Gone to Rome to blow out that Candle."

THE PENGUIN STORY

A Torontonian was on his way to the zoo with two hundred penguins in his truck. He experienced some mechanical trouble and had pulled onto the shoulder of the highway and was there for a considerable time. A Newfoundlander was going by in his truck and noticed the Torontonian. He stopped and got out of his truck and asked him. "What's d'trouble old cock?" Reply. "I'm taking two hundred penguins to the zoo and my truck has broken down". The Newfoundlander said, "B'y, my truck is as big as yours, lets put 'em in my truck. I'll take them to the zoo". The Torontonian was very pleased, transferred the penguins and gave the Newfoundlander $200.00 to take them to the zoo.

Fine. About ten o'clock that night the Torontonian was walking down Yonge Street and saw the Newfoundlander coming up the street with the two hundred penguins following him.

Torontonian: Hey Buddy, I told you to take those penguins to the zoo.

Newfoundlander: I took them to the zoo. You gave me $200.00 and I have some left over, so now I'm taking them to the movies.

TURNIPS ARE KEPT IN THE CELLAR

The Magistrate had held court in the school house. The trial of Joe was over. Joe had been proven guilty beyond doubt. He had stolen on three occassions from the general store. The plaintiff was amazed when the Magistrate had ruled a suspended sentence.

Magistrate: You can't get blood from a turnip.

Plaintiff: No. But you can put it in the cellar for thirty days.

'TIS NOT GOOD TO BE DOIN' NUTTIN'

Very recently I was told about a skipper and his two sons who were rowing up the arm in a stiff breeze of wind. The wind became steadily worse and eventually the skipper said to row in behind an island which was to their port side, and get in the lun.

After about two hours idleness, the skipper got feeling steadily worse, thinking about all the time the three of them were losing and nothing getting done. This got to him and he said to the boys to haul the boat out into the arm once more.

DON'T ASK TOO MANY QUESTIONS:

There had been ten children in the family, boys & girls. One of the girls, a friend of mine, was chiding her mother for having so many offspring. She was telling her mother how much easier life would have been for her had she only had three or four.

Then in a very light hearted vein she said, "Mother, if someone had come to you and offered to take all of us off your hands except one, which one would you have kept? Without hestitation her mother came back with, "It would have been too bad for you. You wouldn't have stood a chance."

NO DOUBT ABOUT IT.

One character in the Village, whom I won't name, had never accomplished much in his life time nor did he accumulate much.

But one morning on the wharf he announced to a group of about ten people, that he had enough money to last him the rest of his life.

That information was passed on to the merchant from whom our friend had received considerable credit. The merchant hit him with, "Tom they tell me you have enough money to last you the rest of your life?" Tom replied, "Yes skipper, if oi lives till tonight."

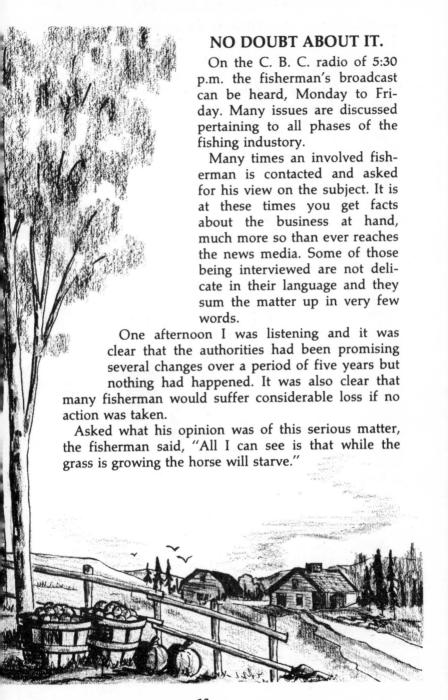

NO DOUBT ABOUT IT.

On the C. B. C. radio of 5:30 p.m. the fisherman's broadcast can be heard, Monday to Friday. Many issues are discussed pertaining to all phases of the fishing industory.

Many times an involved fisherman is contacted and asked for his view on the subject. It is at these times you get facts about the business at hand, much more so than ever reaches the news media. Some of those being interviewed are not delicate in their language and they sum the matter up in very few words.

One afternoon I was listening and it was clear that the authorities had been promising several changes over a period of five years but nothing had happened. It was also clear that many fisherman would suffer considerable loss if no action was taken.

Asked what his opinion was of this serious matter, the fisherman said, "All I can see is that while the grass is growing the horse will starve."

CAMPUS HUMOR

When we talk about folklore humour it must be said that one student at Memorial University, who comes from the outports, can bring more sense and humour to the class room, than a dozen city fellers.

If you will read the following happenings which took place at Memorial University a few years back, they will verify the foregoing statement.

A young lady in the graduating class came to see one of her instructors and told him she was trying to get a teaching position. As of that date she had not been offered the sort of thing in which she was interested.

The instructor, who knew the girl to be an excellent student, asked her, "What sort of teaching work interests you?"

"Well sir, she said, I wants to teach in a culturally deprived h'area."

"That is a wonderful desire", said the teacher. "I hope you get just such an opportunity. Where would you like to do this sort of work?"

To which she replied: "Sin Jan's".

After a test in an introductory course on the christian faith a student approached his instructor and said: "Sir, I answered that first question in terms of the Messiah, alright?"

The instructor replied: "No, my son, there's no way you could answer that first question in terms of the Messiah."

"Well Sir, said the student, look again at the question Sir, I think it could be so interpreted that it could be answered in terms of the Messiah."

"I'm sorry" said the instructor, "but that question could not possibly be answered in terms of the Messiah."

"Right you are", said the student, "I agree with you, in which case I plead for mercy".

(As it turned out he was wise to plead for mercy. It was only through the mercy of the instructor he was passed).

GARBAGE!

A lady had gotten an early start on her preparation for an evening out.

Her hair was up in curlers which were sticking off from her head in all directions. The first stage of a facial had been just completed, which consisted of having her face covered with a grayish, muddy looking material.

At this point she heard the approach of the garbage truck. She donned her house coat and in the same motion hurried down over the flight of steps to the side walk, and announced,

GOOD REASONING

A chap had searched many months in his effort to find employment. Since he had been layed off he answered many ads appearing in the employee want section of the newspapers.

One day there was an ad which interested him very much and he rushed to tell his wife he knew he could get this job. She asked him why he was sure and he replied, "This ad says that, 'the successful applicant must be responsible.' In every job I ever had, and anything went wrong, I was responsible."

VIGOUR WINS SOULS

In a certain community of Newfoundland, a new Salvation Army officer had been assigned to the local barracks. One of the members was not too happy with the new man and was giving his opinion to his United Church friend, in a very voluable manner and in no uncertain terms.

The new feller didn't do a good job of preaching. He wasn't forceful enough. The previous captain in his loud voice could shout loud enough, throw his arms around and pound the desk enough to scare the devil out of anyone.

His friend agreed and said that he was not too pleased either with the new minister at his church for the same reason. But then he added, "Ah well H'Uncle 'Arry, I guess 'tis as me old fauder used to say, tis not always the pig that squeals the loudest makes the best bacon."

DID YOU EVER GO TO SCHOOL?

I think that back, say fifty or sixty years ago, people were not frowned upon if they did not go to school. It surely proved quite a handicap in later years no doubt, but was not looked upon as a disgrace. His or her education was along practical lines, the kind that would bring income to the family unit now, be that income ever so small.

Some years after Confederation, Ottawa personel were interviewing older citizens of our island province. These people were endeavouring to find out how far reaching our illiteracy was. Now some people have a hard time answering questions with one or two words. Their answer has to be in the form of a story, short or long.

One gentleman to be interviewed was a survivor of the Newfoundland Disaster of 1914. He was the late Mr. Cecil Mouland. He told this story himself.

Interviewer: Mr. Mouland, how long were you in school?

Mr. Mouland: Well now zir, the first day I was in school they were readin' 'bout Tom and his dog. Someone threw a stick out into the pond, and Tom's dog went after it. Before Tom's dog was back to shore I was out of school.

THE GHOST DRIVER

About thirty years ago I was visiting the home of a friend who lived in Conception Bay. During the evening we had spent some time discussing the preference we had for different makes of cars. Then the discussion turned to garages and repair men.

He explained that he always took his car to a local fellow, and he mentioned his name. I had never heard of him. He explained that the fellow he was talking about was very short and only about 3 feet tall. He started to explain further then he stopped and said, "Look, if you see an old "Model T" Ford goin' up the road and nobody drivin' it, that's Sandy Candow."

WHAT'S IN A NAME

The Minister to whom this happened told me the following story.

He was living in an area where his parish was rather spread out. He received a call late one night to come to the home of one of his parishoners, and he was needed urgently.

When he arrived at the home, which was five miles away, he learned that a baby had been born that evening. He also learned that the doctor had given the parents very little hope of the baby's living more than a few hours.

The urgent call to the Minister was the fact that they wished to have the baby baptized right away. It was evident that the man and his wife were having difficulty deciding on a name. Eventually he turned to the Minister and said in haste, "Reverend, waze your name?" "Ephraim." Disapprovingly he turned to his wife and said, "Ephraim, Ephraim. Dat's good enough. Let's call en dat. Ee's not gonna live long h'anyway.

18

THE ANTIQUE COLLECTOR

I have heard of many stories about antique collectors who came to Newfoundland shortly after Confederation. These individuals had a hey day for Newfoundland was a collector's paradise. There were houses full of very old handmade furniture and thousands of precious old china, crystal and glass.

The collectors knew the dollar value of these antiques. But the unfortunate fact is that many unscrupulous ones paid the owners only a fraction of the worth of each item.

Here, however, is a story of a very horrified antique collector. He was a clever fellow so he went into the barn to have a look around before going to the home of one of the older residents. To his delight he saw an old table that was worth at least $200.00. No doubt it had been layed aside in favour of one of our modern flashy looking chrome sets.

WHEN THE COLLECTOR RETURNED

19

WHAT'S YOUR CAPACITY?

I have heard many descriptive remarks when people have refered to men who had an unusual capacity for alcoholic beverages.

Last week we were discussing a certain individual when my mother-in-law remarked, "DRINK? Yes he'd drink the sea dry and walk home be land."

WORSE THAN EMBARRASED

Some years ago, I spent an evening listening to the experiences of a teacher who had taught in the outports for many years. One story he told was rather humourous but not so for one unlucky and timid student.

It appears there were two schools involved and there was an area between th two schools which was rather a "no-man's land". All students of both schools had been warned not to enter this territory.

One afternoon, just after lunch break, the principal of one of the schools noticed a boy in this no-man's-land and ordered him to his office. The boy complied and after a good lecture the student was given five hard whacks on each hand. Then the principal asked sharply, "Who is your teacher and what class are you in?" The boy replied "Sir, Sir, I don't go to this school."

BROTHERLY LOVE.

Two brothers from the Northern Peninsula went to Corner Brook and bought a pretty dilapidated car for about three hundred dollars. They managed to get it home and then the next piece of business was for each brother to get his drivers licence.

An appointment was made with the local R.C.M.P. detachment and only one brother turned up for his test. The R.C.M.P. officer got in and told the boy to proceed down the road. After about a quarter of a mile he realized he was in a car which was not fit to be on the road. It was a real hazard to all other drivers on the highway.

R.C.M.P. Officer: My gosh b'y! this car is a menace, and you are a menace to be driving a car in this condition. What about if you were coming down that steep hill over there and your brakes gave out?

Driver: Never mine 'bout dat b'y, me brudder 'll be driving 'er den.

DESPERATION!

A young couple had made several futile attempts to get themselves married on a Saturday afternoon. Neither of them wished to be married by a Justice of the Peace. They had been around to the Anglican priest, the United Church minister, and the Salvation Army major. At each parish residence they got the same answer: "No. You must have a marriage licence."

In desperation he returned to his first try, the Anglican priest. But the answer was still no. In further desperation he looked at the Anglican priest and said, "Now look 'ere b'y Rev., can't you say a few words just to get us over the weekend?"

WIVES ARE HARD TO PICK OUT.

Three monthe after I had been married in October 1976, I met a friend while shopping at the Avalon Mall.

While we chatted he asked me how my new married life was getting along. I told him that things were just fine and gave him an optomistic view of the future. In answering I had also explained in jest, that I had waited six years and it had taken me all that time to pick her out.

He replied that he was thirty-six years old before he got married.

I asked him why it had taken him so long to make a choice of a wife and he said, "I knew what I *wasn't* looking for."

WHAT'S SUFFICIENT?

In a certain area of Newfoundland, about twenty years ago, it was necessary to expropriate land for a government project. Some of the land owners were quite disturbed over losing their land. It was decided to have a meeting in the school house with a government official to explain and discuss the problems arising.

The official talked for a considerable time and now and then he would say that there was no need to worry that everyone would get sufficient for their land. Then he stopped to ask if there were any questions and the following ensued:

"DEECIPLES ON SAY GALALAY"

Uncle Charlie Wimbleton lived in Springdale, Notre Dame Bay. Uncle Charlie was retired by the time he told this story. He had a very retentive memory and an imaginative mind and could relate stories that provided entertainment for all who knew him.

Uncle Charlie loved to paraphrase the scriptures in his own special way. He would go to church on Sunday and hear the scriptures. Then on Monday he would relate the particular parable he had heard in church yesterday.

Before Confederation we had the Rangers who were the law keepers in our outports. The late Roy Manuel was the Ranger in Springdale at the time and he met Uncle Charlie and heard the following story.

Uncle Charlie: Ranger you wouldn't to church yistidy mawning.

Ranger: No Uncle Charlie I had to go on a cruise for the Force.

Uncle Charlie: Well Ranger if youse wuz along wid we in Church yistidy, youse a 'eard d'Riverend Carnell talkin' 'bout d'deeciples on Say Galalay.

Peter, James and John wuz along an' day wuz out dere all night but never got a zign. Nar feesh a'tall look. 'Long 'bout dawn dey 'eard a feller bawlin' at 'em from d'beach. An' Ranger, James said, 'Dats d'blessed Master'. An' wid dat Peter went slowze overboard. E'd drowned if James an' John 'adn't been dere to 'aul en een.

Den d'blessed Master bawled at 'em an 'h'asked 'em what um wuz doin' out dere. Dey said, 'Master we've a bin 'ere all night an got neara feesh. Nar one'. An' d'blessed Master bawled at en Ranger, an' said, 'Cartny b'ys youse got no feeh youse got d'nit on wrong side punt, look'. Well Ranger dey 'auled en een an'chucked en out d'hudder side. An' Feesh! My zon! Dey Vulled d'cuddy, an' dey vulled en aft, an eef dey 'ad anudder punt dere dey would a vulled ee too. Den dey 'ad anudder spell feeshin' an' den dey pulled d'punt ashore. An' while dey wuz puttin' away dere feesh d'blessed Master cooked en up a pot a feesh an' brewis.

YOU'D BE NO DIFFERENT

The telephone service did not come to all areas at once. It came to cities first of course and gradually got to the rural parts of countries.

It was also a fact that older people were quite timid in answering this new fangled thing and often were too nervous to answer it for the first month or so.

I was told about one old gentleman who lived alone and who's daughter had insisted that he have the telepone installed. This was done so she could call him regularly to enquire about his health and have a chat with him so he would not be lonely.

The phone was installed alright but the old man gave it a wide berth for several weeks.

One night when it rang he let it go on for about five minutes and then ran to it with a vengenance, pulled the receiver from the hook on the old time telephone box and yelled, "THERE IS NO ONE HERE CAN TALK," and replaced the receiver on its hook with a bang.

LIFE INSURANCE AT 70

People who retain their sense of humour over the years are always welcome in any society.

I knew a lady who never failed to give me a good laugh while I was in her company. I was talking to a life insurance agent when this particular lady came into his office. She was seventy years old at the time.

In fun he took out an application form for life insurance and asked her questions about herself pertaining to her being accepted for a policy on her life. When he came to the question—"Have you had any serious illnesses or operations that might prevent you from obtaining life insurance?"—She replied, "How about twelve pregnancies?"

SUPPORT FOR THE MICS

Overheard in a St. John's bar at 3:30 A.M.

A man ordered a drink and when the waitress brought the bill there was quite a fuss.

PATRON: Look here you ain't charging me ($5.00) for one shot of whiskey are ya?

WAITRESS: Well sir, the charge is $3.50 for the liquor and $1.50 for the mix.

PATRON: WHAT! ARE YOU CROWD SUPPORTIN' DEM TOO?

GOD LIVES IN STRANGE PLACES

A Sunday School superintendant asked all the gathering of children, where does God live?

He received no reply for several seconds and then one young fellow ventured,

EARS ARE IMPORTANT

The following was given to me as a true story, but true or not 'tis good for a laugh, especially for carpenters.

A carpenter was working from the scaffold on the construction of a new building. A story above him a metal roof was being installed. A piece of the metal was on it's way to the ground and it hit the carpenter on the side of the head chopping off his ear. He hurried to the ground and started to look for the ear in the light fall of snow. He refused to leave for the hospital until he found the ear. A couple of others joined in the search, soon the ear was recovered and the finder said excitedly, "Here it. Here it is!" The carpenter looked at it quickly saying, "No b'y, no b'y, dat's not me h'ear, my h'ear 'ad a pencil in en."

HIS JUDGEMENT WAS RIGHT ANYWAY
SALVATION ARMY

A woman in one of our outports had heard the visiting major preach in a very voluable and noisy manner. His subject was, Sin, Repentance and Judgement day.

All the major said kept getting to her while in the barracks, on the way home, and before she went to bed, and while lying in bed before she went to sleep.

At three o'clock in the morning she was awakened with the noise of thunder and lightening. She lost touch with reality and in her fright she woke her husband excitedly almost shouting, "JOE. JOE. GET UP. GET UP. 'TIS JUDGEMENT DAY!" It was very dark so he said, "Yer fullish maid! Yer fullish! What next! What next! Judgement day, middle of d'night!"

DANCIN'!

In February of this year I visited Hawaii. Can you imagine my picking up a funny folklore story about Newfoundland in Hawaii? Well, I did.

I was visiting a lady from the Southern Shore who now lives in one of those beautiful islands.

I told her one or two of my stories relative to the Southern Shore and she said, "Well, I'll tell you one now. Dere's a fella up d'shore an' he's very, very short an' he's a great step dancer. His favourite at a toime, is to wait till everyone is off d'floor and get out an' give a one man show. He can dance, as you'd say, dance rings around anyone.

Well, one night he was especially spry and givin' it all he had. So I said to Dad, "Dad b'y, Paddy is goin his height tonight! And Dad said, "Well Pat girl, dat's not much trouble. Paddy doesn't have to go far to jump the height of himself!"

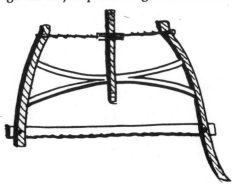

WHAT ELSE COULD IT BE?

I was telling one of the older post office clerks a story. He listened and then laughed a little and told me it was a true story. He remembered the character.

A number of years ago there was a postal clerk who smoked cigarettes, and of course there is nothing unusal about that. But what was unusual was the fact that when the cigarette became quite short and the fire was near his his lips, he stuck a pin into it to get a few more draws from it.

One day in the lobby of the old General Post Office a newsboy asked the man if he wanted to buy a paper. The man did not answer, so the boy asked again but still no answer. On the boy's third request the man said, "No", very rudely. The newsboy looked up at him and seeing just about nothing of a cigarette, then said, "Mister, yer chaw of backie is on fire."

FIGURE IT OUT FOR YOURSELF

Tom Quinlan is an Englishman who has done his share of world travelling. and spent his recent years in Newfoundland working as a columnist.

In April, 1968 Tom was on the C.B.C. program "Between Ourselves". When he was asked to pass his opinion on the Newfie Jokes told by upper Canadians he said, "I've travelled around the world quite a bit and I've heard jokes told in Australian pubs, Indian tea shops, South American Bazaars and I've even heard the odd joke told in Ontario".

CAN YOU READ A PRESCRIPTION?

Some years ago two fellows lived in Bonavista. They were quite good friends but neither could read.

One of them had reason to go to the doctor and the doctor gave him a prescription. On his way home he met his friend and showing him the prescription said, "John: Do you know what's on this prescription"? George: "You knows b'y, oi don't know how to read. But let me 'ave a look at en. Look b'y, all dem prescriptions are missages from the doctor to the druggist an' dey say, 'I got mine, now you get yours'".

THE PATRON SAINT

Forty years ago I was a young Kinsmen. The late Dr. Louis Conroy was the first president of that organization in Newfoundland.

I was on the executive and enjoyed the stories of the older men who were also members.

I should precede the story I wish to tell, by saying the Southern Shore is that part of Newfoundland's coast line, which stretches from St. John's to Cape Race. It is an extablished and well documented fact, that for many years that area had its quota of ship wrecks and many lives were lost. Very few of those ships that went on the rocks were ever salvaged. The high seas which were the cause of the wrecks in the first place, made short work of ships that went ashore.

The men of the various communities on the shore always did what they could to rescue any of the crew who survived by clinging to what was left of the wreck.

However, it is also true that the men in those communities always consided that it was only sensible to board these wrecks and remove from the remains what was movable.

Enough had gone to the bottom already. It was also a case of first come first served, and they served themselves. Proper ting!

Many and varied, large and small, were the prizes removed from these wrecks. Anything drinkable, liquor of course (not Carnation) saw sudden death. Many of the items were a first to arrive on the Southern Shore. I mean that there were some items it was difficult to determine their use. Also there were items that people had difficulty determining their significance. It is about one of these items I now wish to relate. An item about which the people became a little confused.

Dr. Conroy related that he journed to Tor's Cove to spend a few days holiday with Rev. Father Coady. The first evening he was there, a knock came to the door and a man asked to see the Doctor Conroy. Louis said, "how they knew I was there I don't know". The man requested Louis to come up to his house, because his wife was having a baby and she was in great trouble. Louis informed him he was there on a holiday and not to bother him.

About an hour passed and the man came back again. Louis said, "no" once more, but the man was not to be put off.

Eventually, he felt that probably he was wrong, and the woman was in trouble and the humane thing to do, since he was in the area, was to go and examine the situation.

The man led him to the wharf and he boarded a large fishing skiff. They steamed along shore for about half an hour and then the man steered the boat into a small cove, all done in the dark.

Next they walked up a short incline to a small three room house. Kerosene lamps were burning because electricity had not come to the shore up to that time. He made an examination and it was quite easily diagnosed as a normal birth. However, he knew she would soon be delivered and he might as well stay and see the poor woman and baby through the ordeal.

He retired to the kitchen to wait. While waiting he noticed a curious thing was happening in the bedroom. Each time the woman had a labour pain, the midwife would grab an object off the bureau and jamb it into the woman's hands and she would pray away until the pain subsided. Then the same thing would be repeated at the next labour pain.

The time arrived when Louis knew it was time for him to officiate. He went into the bedroom, delivered the baby and returned to the kitchen after washing. He was about to leave but returned to the bedroom to ask what had been placed in the hands of the woman in the bed, when she was experiencing the labour pains. The midwife spoke up and said,

"Oh Doctor, Doan't ya know what dat is? Dat's d'patron saint of d'labour pains."

Louis said, "I've been a Catholic all my life but I had never heard of the patron saint of the labour pains. I picked up the object and took it near the lamp to have a close look. Blessed God! It was a bust of Beethoven."

GRADE SEVEN

It was the period in the school schedule when Grade VII had a lesson on religion. The teacher was doing the best he could on the subject of eternity. Getting near the end of the period and wanting to see how well he had done, he asked the students what their understanding of eternity was. One girl of twelve spoke up and said, "Well sir, last Christmas Dad bought a new chesterfield and when Mom came from the H.F.C. last week, she said that the way she was paying it off, it would take till eternity."

SHE KNEW THE DIFFERENCE

Mrs. Tomkins of Doyles in the Codroy Valley, said there was a young Irish priest in the valley when her children were young. Every time he visited he gave the youngest child a quarter.

Monsignor Kerwin, accompanied the young priest one afternoon when he came to see the family.

All the family and the Reverend gentlemen were in the living room with everyone on their best behaviour. The little girl who always got the quarter became impatient and went and stood in front of the young priest and said, "Gimme some money". She said nothing to the child not expecting her to do it again. But she did. When she said gimme some money a second time the old Monsignor put his hand in his pocket and pulled out a nickel offering it to the child saying. "There my dear and what do you say?" "Gimme some more".

THE CITY DWELLER

Having acquired a new wife in 1976, I now spend my summer vacation, along with her, of course, at the Codroy Valley which was where Mary grew up. You know, 'tis quite conventient to be married to an outport person because, as I have discovered, when it comes vacation time there is no need of reservations and the grub is free. For a person like myself it has been quite interesting and real fun to listen to the folklore of the Valley, and to be sure, the Codroy is about the nicest place in Newfoundland to spend a holiday.

Now, over the years I have done considerable cooking, nothing professional now, but passable home cooked meals for the family, along with the odd cake and pan of cookies. For this reason, while at my in-laws domicile, I am called upon to be the cook for the main meal of the day. You see my brother-in-law is developing a small fruit farm, and just when we arrive there, all help possible is needed for gathering the crop, especially the strawberries. Everyone has to do something on those occasions. Nobody is HAULED off on the settle.

Being the oldest of those eating off the house, they spared me the back-breaking stooping over the plants. "Just have the meals ready and on time, that's all," is what I am told with warning tone. Well, I suppose its worth it for we do get a few crocks of strawberry jam out of the hassle, that's if we put on the pot.

Well one day, I had just put the salt junk in the pot for dinner, when I said to Lew, "what greens are we having?" he described the area of the garden where the swiss-chard was and described the swiss-chard also. I guess I was not listening too well that day, when I rounded the corner of the house he was right there. He looked at the greens and exploded, "THAT"S NOT SWISS-CHARD! YOU'VE PICKED THE LEAVES OFF MY PUMP-KINS!" (Really now, if a fellow only knew, there is not much resemblance, is there?) I thought I had ruined his pumpkins but there is one thing that saved them. It appears I had been listening to one thing he said. He had instructed me to pick only a few leaves from each plant of the swiss-chard and I only picked a few leaves from each plant of his pumpkins.

The plants survived and we did manage to get a pumpkin out of it in the fall for ourselves.

City dwellers are some stun!

The Author

A NEWFOUNDLANDER'S DEGREES OF PAIN

An Englishman who worked with Bowaters in Corner Brook made this remark. "It is very difficult for me to understand many Newfoundlanders but I have learned one thing, that there are three degrees of pain in Newfoundland.

THE PRICE OF HEAVEN

A wealthy parishoner had always given most generously to his church, in fact he was the best giver of all the members in his church. In fun he had always claimed that his givings would assure him of his getting into heaven.

Not being sure of how much he would have to give to accomplish such a feat, he wondered out loud, in the presence of his clergyman, just how much more he would have to give to make sure. Jokingly, the clergyman promised he would pray about the matter and try and get the answer.

Some days later the clergyman met the fellow and told him that he had the answer. It would cost him another $10,000.00 but there was something else. "What's that?" the wealthy man asked. "Be Ready Friday."

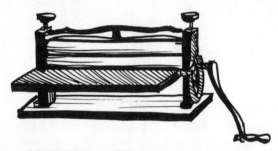

HARD TO BELIEVE BUT TRUE

A general merchant told me about a man who lived in country some miles from the community. He eked out a living by working at several occupations. He fished, cut logs, trapped a bit and worked for people by the day.

One day in the store he picked up a few items and then said to the merchant, "Skipper, 'ow much would youse pay for a silver fox?" "Forty dollars I suppose", was the reply. "Can I 'ave some credit?" "Yes, OK". The fellow then picked out about forty dollars worth of groceries and merchandise and left.

Six months passed and yet no sign of the trapper nor the silver fox.

One afternoon the merchant was looking out the store window when he spotted the man down the road. He sent his clerk after him and without hesitation he returned with the clerk.

Merchant: "I gave you $40.00 worth of credit. Where's the fox?"

Trapper: "Sure ol' man, I never tol' ee I 'ad en. I h'asked you 'ow much would you pay fer en."

AS LONG AS YOU KNOW WHAT YOU MEAN

About twenty-five years ago a certain performer was supposed to show up at the radio station in St. John's to rehearse for his weekly show, which was on that evening. It was pretty customary that if he did not show by three o'clock some of the staff were sent out to look for him.

There were eight or ten well known establishments at which it was likely to find the singer. All the searching failed this particular day but one of the staff returned with the following news. He had gone to one hideout and one fellow had seen him that morning. Asked what he thought his condition was he said, "Well if you ask me I'd say he was 'alf abrievated".

BROWN TOAST

A salesman told me about going into a small restaurant with two of his friends and ordered their breakfast.

The ordering was completed and the waitress was walking away when he said, "Oh yes, and I'll have brown toast!" The waitress came back to their table and said, "Look 'ere, we puts 'en in da toaster an' eh toast 'en. An' dat's da way you'll git en".

37

KEEP AN EYE ON YOUR GIRL FRIEND

When talking about the old Newfoundland Railway, the station at Goobies was referred to often by ardent anglers. Today it is referred to more often as the point at which you depart from the Trans Canada Highway and proceed down the highway to the Burin Peninsula.

Two years ago I arrived at Goobie's at 2:00 P.M. I was on my way to Grand Bank and stopped for a lunch at the Irving Service Station. After telling a couple of stories one of the ladies on the staff at the restaurant told me this story.

She said that last night a fellow stopped his car at the gas pump, told the attendant to fill the tank and then he proceeded to the washroom. He then came from the washroom, paid for the gas, got aboard his car and drove off.

Two hours later when he arrived in town and stopped at his mother's home, he opened the rear door of the car and told his girl friend to wake up, they were in St. John's. But, no girl friend was there. What a surprise. What happened?

At Goobies when he had gone to the washroom she was in the back of the car asleep. But she woke up, and also went to the washroom. He did not know this and proceeded on his way without her.

When he realized what had happened he drove right back to Goobie's, 100 miles. When he arrived back there, he was told she had left an hour before on the C.N. bus.

REMEMBERING, THE POLITICIANS DILEMA

On one of Joey Smallwood's forays into the Bay, he stepped on the wharf and saw about two hundred citizens of the settlement. They had turned out early in the morning to greet their premier, (or priemier, I prefer premier).

Well the local Liberal Nabob was on hand to also greet his premier (or priemier) and a lot of hand shaking was about to commence.

As the nabob and premier (or priemier) advanced down the line of faces, Joey was asking under his breath who each one was, in order to greet the supporter by his first name. Of course Joey greeted each one as an acquaintance of some years.

One man he greeted was a fellow by the name of John Henry. Joey asked about his family and particularly his wife. John Henry replied by saying she had died and went into some detail as to her ailment. As you can imagine Joey was not too interested, so he moved on to the next fellow and eventually he shook the right hand of all two hundred faithful.

It was late afternoon when Joey returned to the boat to continue his voyage of conquering. A few men were still on the wharf and one of them was John Henry. Joey approached him not remembering he had met John Henry that morning.

NO MORE ARGUMENT

A couple of fellows from St. Mary's Bay were discussing two well known fishing skippers of that bay. Each one had his hero and was vigorously defending the abilities and skills of his champion.

In time the discussion turned into an argument which terminated as follows: One said to the other, "Lookut, skipper Mike knew where all the rocks are in St. Mary's Bay." To which the other replied "Sure an' dat he did, CAUSE HE HIT "EM ALL".

A LOW BLOW

A few weeks ago, I met an old friend from the bay. We have had many laughs through the years and it is customary for us to start laughing before many words are said. What a relationship! But this is true and with quite a few of my friends this is what happens.

However, my friend from the bay had a story. It is the type of story which you have to imagine you are there and viewing the situation from behind the curtain.

It appears that he went to visit his great uncle. He was not there very long before he felt the atmosphere rather tense. It was evident that uncle and aunt had surely had a disagreement. Words were few and not many of them at all.

When he had been there about half an hour, a knock came to the door, Aunt Mary answered it and a fellow selling encylopedias requested that he come in. Aunt Mary consented and the salesman came into the kitchen where we had been sitting. Right away he started his sales pitch which he followed for about five minutes. Suddenly he realized he would have to use a better approach and kept addressing Aunt Mary more than Uncle John. He made the following statement—"You should have this encyclopedia because when your grand-children come to visit and your nieces and nephews, they will ask questions and any answers you are not sure of you will find in this encyclopedia." Uncle John was not long in interrupting the saleman and made his own statement—"Young man, you're talking to the wrong woman now, cuz H'aunt Mary 'ere KNOWS H'EVERYTHING!"

THE REVEREND VS ISLAND COVE

Not long ago, I was talking to a former resident of Bell Island, Conception Bay. We were talking about the days when the iron ore mines were in full swing. We discussed the fellows who worked there and the communities in the bay from which they all came.

Of course, Upper Island Cove was included and once more I spoke of the great humour of these people and how their humour was hereditary.

This former resident told me a story which had been passed on to him by the Reverend Legge, now Bishop Legge.

Reverend Legge had two Island Cove fellows painting a house for him at Lance Cove. He went to see how they were doing one morning and thought he would kid them a little. REVEREND LEGGE: "Boy's, you have done a good job, but on the eastern end, which you just finished, the paint is on inside out." Without hesitation, one of the men said in reply, "Yes sir, we knows dat, and now we're waitin' fer 'en to dry so we can turn 'en over.

SAUCEY TEETH

Ted Skakum is a denturist who practices his profession on the south west coast of Newfoundland.

Ted told me about a lady for whom he had made a set of false teeth. When she came to have them fitted she happened to bring along her husband. He asked the man to wait in another room while he did the fitting. At the completion of his work Ted asked the husband to come and see if he approved.

Ted: What do you think of these teeth?

The husband stood in front of his wife and as she stretched her mouth from one side to the other he said: "Do dis,—Now do dis," then he exclaimed. "De're alright as long as de're not as saucy as d'last set she had.

SURE HARD TO PLEASE

A Newfoundlander went into a Toronto barber shop. After the barber had taken some pains to cut his hair as instructed, he indicated that the job was finished and removed the white shroud.

When the Newfoundlander looked in the mirror to examine how good the hair cut was, the barber asked him if he was satisfied. The reply he received was, "It will do till I get to a barber".

HOW DO YOU KNOW IF YOU'RE NOT AN R.C.

In June of this year I met a reverend gentleman who told me the following story.

Before Confederation two Newfoundlanders visited Toronto. Being friendly sort of fellows they saw no reason why they should not give a greeting to everyone just as they did home in their own local community. They received very little response and naturally were annoyed to find people so unfriendly.

However, at one point in their strolling along, a pedestrian did greet them and they found him to be quite amicable. They knew by his suit he was a clergyman so they asked him what denomination he was. He was a Roman Catholic Priest and this surprised them because they had never talked to a R.C. priest in their lives, and they thought it so nice of him to stop and talk with them.

Now the priest had his arm in a sling so they asked him what had happened. He explained to them that getting out of the bath last week he had slipped and fallen and broken his arm. They were quite sympathetic, and told him. In a few minutes they bid the priest farewell and strolled on.

When they got out of earshot of the priest, one of the Newfoundlanders said to the other, "Buttie, what's a bath?" The reply, "B'y, how do you expect me to know, I'm not a Roman Catholic."

43

HOW UNFORTUNATE, NO LICENCE!

A personal acquaintence of mine was visiting Northern Newfoundland and when he came to a certain community he stopped his car and made some enquiries in an attempt to find a relative.

The man he was talking with did not know anyone by that name but he kept on repeating the name to himself. My friend then said his relative was a Mountie. Well, that bit of information triggered his memory for he excitedly said, "Oh yes, he's the fella that sent me to jail for nine months. Yes b'y, I knows eh". My friend then said he was sorry to have reminded him of something so unpleasant. The reply to that was, "B'y, dat's OK b'y. I 'ad a great time down in the prison shur. I worked in the laundry unit look. T'was great in there b'y. I spent half d'time out on d'truck goin' around Sin Jon's. Goin' all over d'place b'y, day after day. One time the truck was parked on Water St. for forty-five (45) minutes an' I was in 'er all alone. The key was in the ignition and d'engine was runnin', an' here was I with nar licence".

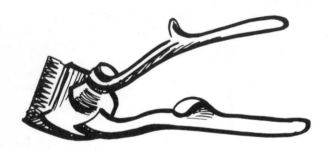

NOT LIKELY

A Newfoundland father decided to make a visit to Toronto to see his son.

After he deplaned at Malton and went to collect his baggage, there was quite a delay before it arrived at the carousel.

In the interval, a man who was standing close to the Newfoundlander, made a number of remarks about the smooth flight, about Air Canada, about the delay, and about a number of other things. It was hardly a conversation. Eventually he said to the Newfoundlander, "Here all your life?" to which our father replied, "I hope not."

LOBSTERS BY D'EACH

My friend Jimmy Martin, who does a great deal of travelling in Newfoundland, told me about wanting to buy some lobsters. He went down to the beach where some lobsters had just been landed. A young fellow had about two hundred in his crate.

BRIDGET BARDOT AND HER NEW BABY

For the past several years a lot has been said about the New-foundland seal fishery.

Years ago, the seal hunt provided a great excuse to philan-thropic organizations to hold a sweep. There were cash prizes for the one holding the ticket having the correct day of the month and the time of day, on which the first steamer arrived back from the hunt. A prize for the holder of the ticket on which was the correct number of seals landed by the S.S. Neptune, S.S. Thetis, S.S. Eagle, S.S. Viking, S.S. Beothic and many others from year to year. Of course, the grand prize was for the total catch. Other prizes were offered for various statistics.

A common expression, amongst Newfoundland sealers, if the voyage was a failure was to say, "Oi loosed me spring." If the voyage was a success then it was, "A Bumper Load".

One sealer who after a poor voyage to the seal fishery that year, journeyed to New York to find work on a construction job. This was quite common in years passed. When he arrived at one construction site the superintendent asked him what he had been doing before he came to New York, and the man replied, "Oi was out to the seal fishery, look; an' Oi loosed me spring." The superintendent asked "What kind of spring did you lose?"

Addressing the Rotary Club in Mississauga last year, I was asked to tell something about the seal hunt. That was quite a chore. With so much being said about the Seal Hunt, how do you mix humour and information on the seal hunt?

I did tell them, however, it was amazing how most of the world had given the seals "souls". Did you ever hear people say baby dogs, baby cows, baby horses, or baby sheep but now to pull heart strings young seals are "baby seals." The next thing we will hear is that Greenpeace will be sending these "Baby Seals" to Sunday School, I told them.

I also told them that Bridget Bardot's picture in the newspa-pers, cuddling a live pup seal, fooled nobody in Newfoundland. I say that because all Newfoundlanders know that if that was a live seal which Bridget was cuddling in that picture, Bridget would be a male actor in her next movie.

HE HAD TO SAY IT

I think it is true to say, that in most smaller communities of Newfoundland, the outports, everyone knows everyone else. It is in those areas that folklore humour evolves.

In 1955, Television first came to Newfoundland and the following story is true folklore humour.

In a certain community on the Southern Shore, television antennas started to stick up from one roof after another. A lady, who was always noted for her fancy hats came to mass one Sunday morning with an exceptionally tall feather sticking up from her hat. One gentleman who was noted for his humourous remarks about anything unusual, went over to this lady after mass and in a very lovely Irish vernacular said to her, "Well, Kit gurl, are ya gittin' a good reciption?"

NERVOUSNESS IS FATAL

A young fellow had successfully completed his high school years in the small community three room school. He made a decision and announced to his mother that he would be leaving to study for the church. This pleased her very much and she was not long in letting others know the good news.

Since this meant his leaving and moving far away from them, many good wishers did what had always been done and it was traditional, a big going away party was held in the Parish Hall and several smaller parties as well. Our prospective candidate for the clergy was on his way.

News of his success in his studies kept filtering back to home and when he was ordained he returned for a holiday before taking up the work of a distant parish to which he had been assigned.

On his arrival home he met the resident minister and of course he thought it would be a good idea if the young minister would give the sermon on Sunday. No Way! How could he stand in the pulpit of the church where he had grown up, and give forth to all these people who had really helped rear him. He refused.

But his mother heard about it and of course her powers over her son prevailed and he consented for her sake.

Now the ancient little church had been rather neglected and had not had as much repairs done to it as should have been. When it came to the sermon on Sunday the resident minister made the announcement that there was no need to introduce the guest preacher, because the people knew the young fellow better than he did.

The young fellow stood in the front of the pulpit and without any preliminaries, he announced his text. "Behold, I Come". After that there was a dead silence. Again he said, "Behold, I Come". but that was as far as he could get. He could not overcome his nervousness, so he moved about a bit and then grabbing the old pulpit and breezing down on it hard, he said once more, "BEHOLD, I COME." Well the old pulpit gave way under his weight and he fell out into the front pews of the congregation and into the arms of the resident minister's wife. He got to his feet and excitedly said to her, "OH, My! I'm so sorry." She replied, "My son, don't worry one bit about it, you warned me three times".

HUMOUR IN RETROSPECT

When preparing this book, I decided to include some of my own life stories which I remember from years back. It is amazing how certain happenings of forty years ago were very serious at the time and looking back they were not like that at all, but very humourous.

The following story is true and relates to an era of Newfoundland history.

In Newfoundland's colonial days (before Confederation), it was customary for our governor, the head of the state, to be sent out from Britain. It was also customary for his personal staff to accompany him. At times, some of these staff members could be very objectionable because of their arrogance.

Sir Humphrey Walwyn, a Vice-admiral of the British Navy was the governor in 1936. His secretary was a Captain Schwerdt, also of the British Navy. This man was uncommonly arrogant.

From 1930 to 1939, I was an employee of Terra Nova Motors. We had as the mechanical foreman a Mr. Richards, who was from London, England. Captain Schwerdt would converse with no one at Terra Nova Motors except the fellow Britisher. On one occassion a special rod was being made for him which would help him navigate the salmon rivers. (If he was a native, he would need no rod.) When he returned to pick up the rod Mr. Richards was out. Cyril Bailey, the fellow who made the rod asked Captain Schwerdt to follow him to his locker. Cyril handed the rod to him saying as he did, "There, sir, you won't fall very often with that rod to help you." The Captain turned on him saying, "Mind your own goddamn business." I always said that this man could have been sired by a prusian general.

I was told that one time during the war he refused to sit down to dinner in the Newfoundland Hotel dining-room until two British ratings, who were off a British Warship in the harbour, were put out of the dining-room. The humour to this story is that after the war, a young red headed Scotsman was manager of the Hotel and when I told him that story, he got so mad he wanted to go looking for Captain Schwerdt right then, ten years after the fact. He said if he was manager he would have offered to throw the captain out instead of the ratings.

October was the year end for Terra Nova Motors. It was always a time to put on a drive to collect accounts. At that time Captain Schwerdt owed us some money which was long over due. Ralph Atwill was with us at the time, and I asked Ralph to call on the captain. Ralph went to the Government House and asked to see Captain Schwerdt, when the captain came out into the vestibule he said in a very abrupt mannor, "Don't you know any better than to come to the front door of Government House?" Without hesitation Ralph replied, "Well Sir, I didn't expect to find you at the back door." Then Captain Schwerdt said, also without hesitation, "And what can I do for you, my son?" In a very British vernacular of course.

That exchange reminds me of a scene from what we years ago called the "funny papers', now the comics. Anyway, I congratulated Ralph and we got payment ten days later.

TIME FOR ANOTHER

Very recently while in the company of the Reverend George Earle, who is a fine story teller, he told the meeting of the H'Anglicans the following:

A man had been on a bender for many weeks. He was out, not knowing night from day. One morning he made a valiant effort to come off the booze. Feeling there was someone close by he said, "Is that the sun or the moon?" The man close by replied "I don't know b'y, I don't belong around here".

THEY HAD NO UNIONS IN BIBLE TIMES

For some years in St. John's, a well known labour union negotiator was a man by the name of Fred Locking.

At Mass one Sunday morning at St. Pius X Parish the Reverend Father Fischer read the Gospel, where the orchard owner paid one worker for one hour's work as much as he paid another worker for eight hour's work.

Coming out of Mass one parishoner was overheard to say to another: "'Twas alright for that orchard owner, but he didn't have Fred Locking to deal with."

THE BEWILDERED PATIENT

There are certain individuals who repeat what they think they heard. Recently a doctor related the following incident that happened at his office. Part of the conversation went this way:-

WOULD YOU BELIEVE?

A visitor to Newfoundland was travelling on the old "Newfie Bullet". After he had performed his morning schedule of washing, shaving and brushing his teeth, he gathered up all his implements of repair and proceeded back to his section of the pullman. As he placed his implements in his case he realized he had left his tooth-brush in the washroom. Arriving back at the washroom he discovered a man using his tooth-brush and said in surprise, "Do you know that you are using my TOOTH-BRUSH?"

Reply, "I'm sorry b'y, I taut it belonged to the C.N.R."

JUST LIKE ISLAND COVE

A visitor was in Island Cove and he was trying to locate a friend who lived there but he had forgotten his name. He tried to describe his friend to one of the residents but without success. Eventually he added one feature which threw some light on the situation when he said, "there is something else I remember about him and that is when he is looking at you it seems his eyes are half shut". The other man then exploded with, "Oh, you must be lookin' fer de feller whose eyes are on low beam all the time."

CAN YOU DRIVE A STANDARD SHIFT?

In 1972 a sales meeting of all agents in the Atlantic Provinces for the Lennox Industries Limited, was held in Dartmout N.S. The meeting place was at the Wandlyn Motel.

One morning about six or seven of us were ordering our breakfast. All orders were taken and the little waitress returned to ask a question about my order. I replied in the affermative by saying "I allow." She said, "I beg your pardon sir," and my reply was, "You're not a Newfoundlander." To my surprise she said, "I certainly am."

Well, I was rather annoyed with myself because I seemed to have embarrassed her to some degree.

The next morning when I entered the dining room there was nobody but the little waitress from yesterday. I said I was sorry about yesterday but she said not to be concerned about it.

Then I proceeded and asked her where her home was in Newfoundland and she said St. John's. What street? Cook's Street. What is your name? Wilson. I stopped there and looked at her for about three or four seconds and then I said, "I got your grandfather his licence, but I told Campbell Mac Pherson he would never learn to drive."

Miss Wilson laughed hearlily and said, "I don't know who you are sir, but you're absolutely right."

Back in the days when I taught people to drive, there was only the standard shift. The clutch was a mystery to some people and they thought it should be removed.

It was eventually because the automatic gear box came along.

FAST HUMOUR

There are very funny people in Newfoundland and of course that is what this book is all about. I mean that it does not matter what the circumstances are, some people can think of the funniest things to say without hesitation.

For about three months a father had been complaining to his fellow employees about his daughter's boy-friend. He had a number of objections to the fellow but his biggest objection was that he was very short.

Eventually one of his friends asked just how short was he. "Well, if he was standing on a chair by the door, he could look through the key-hole with both eyes."

Another instance of the same sort of thing was a man who had been talking about his deceased friend. He was asked how long his friend had been dead. He tried to explain without giving any specific date but got rather confused. In his frustration he said, "I'll tell ya, now, if he had lived till next September he'd be dead three years".

BANANAS

A woman came home from the supermarket and as her husband came into the kitchen, he could not believe it, bananas were everywhere.

Husband: What are you doing with all these bananas?

Wife: Well, they were on sale—all you wanted for a dollar. So I bought $3.00 worth.

RIGHT ON

A middle aged man was about to have a heart transplant. The evening before the operation, the chief surgeon visited his patient and said, "Now, Michael, you are a very fortunate fellow. This is most unusual but you are to have a choice of three hearts. One is from a beautiful blonde, who has won a number of beauty contests, or a heart from a nuclear physicist, who has accomplished a lot in his work, or a heart from a banker, a banker who has gone from sweeping the floor to being the President. You have the night to think it over."

In the morning the surgeon returned. "Well, Michael, have you made your choice?" Michael replied, "Yes doctor, the banker." "Why the banker?" asked the doctor. To which Michael answered, "'Tis highly probable, it's never been used."

THE DOTTED LINE

A Newfoundlander was driving on the Ontario Highway. His driving seemed to be somewhat erratic. He would speed along quite fast for a quarter of a mile and then slow right up. Then he would go slowly for a few hundred yards then he would take off and speed at seventy or more for probably half a mile, then go into the slow state again.

The police followed him for three or four miles and then they thought they had better get this menace off the road. They directed him to pull into the side which he did.

Police: Look here that's no way to be driving a car, going so fast then slowing up. You are holding up traffic then you take off and drive like crazy.

Newfoundlander: B'y, I have a licence and it says to drive that way.

The Newfoundlander produced his licence.

Police: There is nothing on this that says you are to drive that way.

Newfoundlander: Yes b'y there is. Look down to the bottom, it says, "Tear along the dotted line".

BUILD YOUR OWN COFFIN?

Some years ago it was a common practice for a man to build his own coffin.

A relative of a gentleman in the outports told me about this man who had built his own coffin. It was made about six months when a request was made for the coffin. A neighbor had died suddenly and would he mind if they could have his already made coffin. No problem, and he built another.

This happened three times in a year. On the fourth request he said, "Sure and that you can. I'll never live to use it".

A WARNING TO THE BRIDE

At one time it was quite a common practice in our outports for a young couple to build a house before they got married.

A young fellow who worked for me back in the 1940's told me this story. A relative of his had built his house before he got married and did a very good job on it. The wedding night came along and they were married in the church and the "toime" was held in the school house.

About two in the morning the man and his bride proceeded to the new house. He opened the door and when his bride made a step to enter, she received a shove with just enough force to make her stumble and find herself full length on the floor. The bride got up bewildered and asked, "And what was that for". To which he replied, "That was for nothin', and now, don't you do anythin'."

YOU TRY IT

A Newfoundlander who was residing in Toronto needed about twenty feet of heavy chain. Not living far from the source of supply, he decided to drag it home.

Rather amused at the sight, a Torontonian was quick to ask a few questions.

STAY AWAKE!

In one particular Anglican congregation there was a man who slept through the sermon but somehow always managed to wake a few moments before the preacher concluded.

On one occassion the preacher had been telling about living the good life and it's rewards. As he talked next about hell and it's rewards he got a little emotional and said, "Those who would like to go to hell, STAND UP!"

Our sleeper was just waking up and heard only the last two words "STAND UP". He immediately got to his feet, and noticing that there were only the preacher and himself standing, he said, "I don't know what we are voting on Reverend, but it seems there are only two of us for it".

DID I HEAR CORRECTLY?

A certain wealthy lawyer in St. John's years ago, told his nephew he would mention him in his will.

The nephew became quite an embarrassment to his family and did little to reform.

The uncle's will was being read and the nephew was present listening intently, " ....
and to my nephew, Conrad, whom I said I would mention in my Will, I say, "HI CONRAD!"

THE QUESTION OF AGE

A census taker was proceeding this morning with his routine work, just the same as he had done yesterday.

He came upon a spinster who refused to answer the question pertaining to age. After all other questions had been dealt with he returned to the question of age but received the same stony resistance. Eventually she said,

A CRUISE TO HEART'S EASE

A little known fact about the Clouston family, is its involvement in the fisheries of Newfoundland. My father, John Clouston, became interested in a number of fishing ventures in the early years of the 1900's and was still involved in the 1930's.

He was the first Newfoundlander to ship chilled salmon to mainland Canada. He built and patented in St. John's, Ottawa and Washington the first artificial salt codfish dryer and had the first fish glue factory in Newfoundland in 1908, in Maggoty Cove. (bottom of Temperance St., St. John's).

In 1916 John Clouston built a fish processing factory at Bay Bulls. Electricity for the factory was obtained by damming Bay Bulls Long Pond, and the hydro plant was at the end of the gorge leading down from Long Pond.

It was one such venture that brought me to Little Heart's Ease, Trinity Bay, in December 1929. There were a number of humourous and interesting incidents which happened on that cruise.

At that community my father had built a herring processing plant, and he spent considerable time there. In 1929 when December rolled around, and when it got close to Christmas, my Dad decided he had better return home to St. John's for the festive season or else. Unfortunately my brother, Knox, had to remain at Heart's Ease to keep things going at the herring plant.

Somehow it didn't seem right that my brother should spend all the Christmas holidays without seeing anything of his family. I therefore made a decision to visit him.

On December 26th I boarded the 5 o'clock "express", later called "The Bullet", and went as far as Northern Bight railway station, arriving there at 10:00 pm.

As arranged a gentleman was to meet me there with ee's 'arse and slide, and that ee did. Ee's arse was a large size pony. The slide was two runners with sturdy home made wood work adjoining them. Besides the main frame there were boards affixed to act as floor boards. Sticking up, both fore and aft, were two sticks about three inches in diameter and each stuck up about three feet. They are known as the horns or 'arns.

Well, don't say I didn't have deluxe transportation.

My luggage was lashed fast to the slide and I was told to get aboard. My reserved seat was about three feet long and its edge was three inches in diameter. Did you ever sit on a seat 3" in diameter with no padding except what has grown on your posterior in nineteen years?

It was a beautiful starlit, bitter frosty night. The man told the 'arse to go, and go the 'arse did. With each hand I held on to a 'arn of the slide, and each time we struck a gulch in the road, I took a dive forward but always seemed to land back on my 3" perch which got harder each time we gulched. I thought the railway coach wooden seats were uncomfortable but this was somthing else.

Hillview was our destination which is at the bottom of Sou'—Wes' Arm. Tomorrow I would be taken to Little Heart's Ease, "acrost and out Sou'—Wes' Arm be skeef".

We arrived at Uncle Billy Frost's about midnight and I did justice to a scoff although it was not my habit to load up before retiring. Next I was shown to a bedroom at the top of the house, "d 'h' attic". And again don't say it wasn't cold. There was a feather bed into which had been placed six or seven heated bricks, the heat of which did not dispose of the dampness of a bed which had not been slept in for some months. If you moved a leg which had already heated up a spot, then you had to use up more body heat to start the process all over again to heat another spot.

I have had three experiences of this sort, one that night, one in Harbour Grace in 1933 and one in P.E.I. in 1947. In those days you did not get the flu you "caught cold". I "caught cold" on all three occassions and it was so bad, it had to be some kind of plague. It took many months to shake the chill which I had acquired from those humidified sheets.

Anyway, nothing more happened to me in Hillview other than catching the plague. I was treated with unbelievable hospitality at Uncle Billy's, Miss Avery, Uncle Billy's neice, kept house for him and as the expression goes "she kept a good table", meaning everything was of good quality and cooked correctly.

Next morning I was directed to the house of the man who was to carry me "acrost Sou '—Wes' Arm be skeef". He was a fellow of about twenty who was quite aware of what his committment was for that morning, which was to get young Clouston to Heart's Ease.

I was invited into the kitchen to wait while my friend got himself "in h'arder". Being a townie, I was amazed how he gave his mother orders and directions, of what and where to get each item of clothing he required. "Mudder oi needs a clean h'under shirt, ee's up in d'dresser in me room". "Mudder me jersey's on d'chair in d'all, git 'n". "Git me h'extra socks too and me long boots are out in d'back porch. Carr dem in to me, now". On this went while he sat there and waited for everything to be brought to him.

I have related this experience to more than one outport person, and I was told that in those days, fifty years ago, it was tradition in many areas of Newfoundland that the mother and girls waited on the father and boys.

"WELL, DID YOU EVER!"

My trip down the arm was uneventful. Greetings on arrival at Heart's Ease were affectionate and we were delighted to see one another. I was taken to the Clouston cabin on the side of the hill where I was to bide for the next five days. The chore of cooking was assigned to me, which I was well used to.

I had brought a large goose with me from St. John's. The cooking of that goose was a first for me. I had never cooked one before. Well, I cleaned and dressed it and installed it in the oven, but not soon enough. Supper time came and we knew it was far from cooked. We removed it from the oven and cut from it enough from the outside to satisfy three people. Mr. Hedley Snelgrove came to visit, he was the teacher in those parts. Some cooks won't believe this but that goose saw the oven three times before we were finished with him.

On my third afternoon at Heart's Ease we had some real excitement the S.S. Su Su was plying Trinity Bay at that time carrying mail and freight for the Newfoundland Government. On this afternoon we watched the Su Su steam into the harbour, stick her nose into the ice, and as normally happened, the mailman walked ashore on the ice.

About ten minutes later we heard one awful banging and when we looked out the cabin window we saw the Su Su, but it was as if she was passing by our front door steps. She was so close to us that it appeared we could put our arms out the window and touch her spars with our hands The banging was her bottom hitting the submerged rocks near the shore. A sudden breeze of wind had taken hold of her and before they could get way under her, she was drifting down the harbour. We rushed down the hill to the landwash and one of the crew threw a rope to us and we ran along shore and placed it around a huge boulder. They first tightened the rope and then started slowly paying it out. The effect was that it gradually slowed her pace and the Su Su swung in against the wharf of the herring plant, "an' we sauve 'er".

Relating this story at a later date we were asked why we had not claimed salvage for the Su Su. Our reply was that the old tub was ready for the scrap heap and probably her owners were rather put out with us for saving her anyway.

New Year's Eve rolled around and I set out on the little mail boat to get back to Northern Bight station to join the incoming "express" to St. John's. Well, another unforgettable event occurred. The cabin on the mail boat was none too large. Three or four men and two women jammed into the cabin and started a fire in the little bogey. No matter what we did volumes of smoke filled the cabin and our eyes. If you went out on the deck you would freeze and if you stayed in the cabin it was not cold, but the smoke was an unbelievable inconvenience.

This continued for about half an hour until the men got suspicious. Two young fellows were half lying on the floor of the cabin where the smoke was not quite so dense. But the give away was that these two buckos were doing too much laughing. The smoke pipe was taken down and unjointed. An overall coat had been stuffed into one length of the pipe which prevented the smoke from escaping. Everyone had a great laugh over this. The young fellows most of all. But the men were not annoyed because they could remember days when they did the same thing themselves or probably worse.

Eventually I arrived at Northern Bight station to learn that the "express" was two hours late. Any other news would not be normal. The news on the "express" kept getting later and later. Mr. Jim Stoyles, the station master, was very kind to me. He kept feeding me loaf and strong tea which was hard for me to drink. However, I was better off than most others who had to be out in the waiting room of the station.

The "express" arrived about two in the morning at a time when I was some sleepy. The old creaking disinfectant smelling railway car did not add to my comfort. It was back to the wooden seats again. Sleep was impossible. The traim arrived in St. John's 10:00 am. It was New Year's Morning. Just time enough to get a few hours sleep before keeping my date on New Year's night.

NOTE: When a Newfoundlander says—Don't say it isn't cold! or Don't say we weren't disappointed! or Don't say she isn't good lookin'!—It is our way of using the negative to make the affirmative more positive.

WOULDN'T WE ALL FEEL THE SAME?

One of the best examples of folklore humour is an incident I experienced myself. Now, most of us at one time or another, through poor communication or for some other reason, have not been able to obtain the information we needed in order to proceed farther.

This fellow was in this very same position. On a visit to the Grace General Hospital one morning last year, I was waiting for a taxi. A man entered the hospital and I could see he was not in familiar surroundings, probably his first visit.

He approached the information desk and spent a minute or so talking with the receptionist. When he left her I could see he had not been enlightened by her answers. He walked along the corridor entering two offices and returning again to the corridor looking just as puzzled.

Eventually he went to the emergency desk and somehow the lady there and himself got on the same wave length. She stood up and coming towards me led the man so far, and then pointed to the elevator.

I had never seen this fellow before but I felt for him, and I was about to speak to him when he stopped in front of me and let his frustration explode with, "Ol' Man if I don't soon find d'feller I'm lookin' fer, ME WOUNDS WILL BE ALL' EALED".

A GENTLEMAN

When the Canada Summer games were held in St. John's in 1977, I managed to get to see a couple of football games. (Soccer, it was always football in Newfoundland).

At one of these games, a happy half-drunk kept one of the bleacher areas continually entertained. He strolled back and forth stopping every fifty feet or so to tell that section of the bleachers a funny story. At times he took our minds off the game. At one point, the police wanted to remove him from the scene. But the spectators were having none of that.

In front of my section he stopped and said, "Took a piece of stock out last night. (In old St. John's "a piece of stock" was a girlfriend). Spent fifty dollars. Would have spent more. (he paused) BUT THAT"S ALL SHE HAD.

MY HALF OF THE RUM

This story was told to me by a chap who did not get his share of the bottle of rum.

In a recent general election in Newfoundland, two fellows from Bonavista visited Clarenville. While there, one of the candidates for the election gave them a bottle of rum, a gift to the two of them.

At night, when the game of cards was well under way, one of them went to the cupboard to get the bottle of rum. The bottle was empty. So, he turned to his friend and said, "Where did all the rum go?" The reply, "Well, b'y, my half was on the bottom, so I had to drink your half to get at mine."

RIGHT ON!

A man from over 'Ome had been in the hospital for the first time in his life. The nature of his ailments required that he fast periodically, receiving very little food but also receiving many inconvient and painful tests.

When he arrived home an old friend asked him how he had been treated while in Hospital.

"Well, 'ol man, firse dem fellers treats ya like a dog. Yes zir, jus' like a dog. Dey starves ya mose to deat', h'xays ya an' pokes at ya tru every h'opening in yer martal frame, an' some 'oles dat are not in yer frame.

Den, ol' man a feller comes an' tells ya how bad he feels 'bout poking at ya, an den, dey tries to cure ya, sends ya 'ome an' tells ya to come back in t'ree monts'. Yes zir, jus' like a dog."

WHIZGIGGIN

A university student had asked me to give him a few of the words or sayings of old Newfoundland which are little used today. I gave him what I had, but I kept on trying to obtain a few more for him.

One day on Water Street, I met Val Goodyear. I asked Val about it and he asked me if I had ever heard of Whizgiggin. I said "no", so then he said "Many times I got the back of my grand-father's hand for whizgiggin'". If you can imagine the following scene, you will learn what whizgiggin' is.

Here are four or five adults sitting in an outport kitchen, having what they consider a sensible discussion on one or two topics of the day, mostly about politics, cartny. Then, over in the corner are two or three children giggling and laughing about really nothing.

It is disturbing to the adults so the grand-father leans over the back of his chair at the same time reaching towards the children and making a rather mild swipe at them, says, "STOP YER WHIZGIGGIN'."

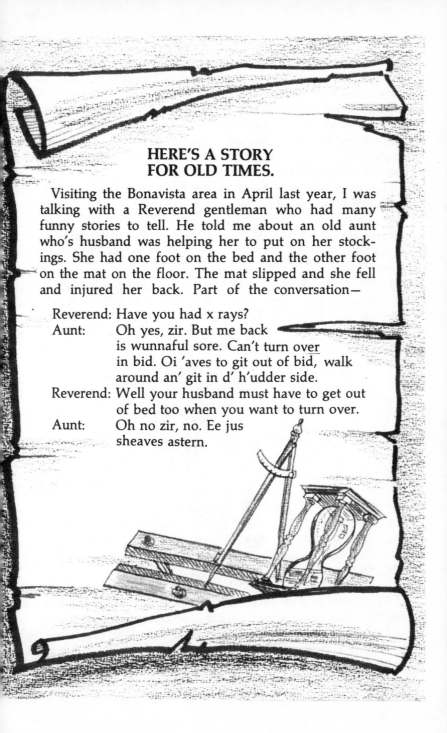

HERE'S A STORY
FOR OLD TIMES.

Visiting the Bonavista area in April last year, I was talking with a Reverend gentleman who had many funny stories to tell. He told me about an old aunt who's husband was helping her to put on her stockings. She had one foot on the bed and the other foot on the mat on the floor. The mat slipped and she fell and injured her back. Part of the conversation—

Reverend: Have you had x rays?
Aunt: Oh yes, zir. But me back
           is wunnaful sore. Can't turn over
           in bid. Oi 'aves to git out of bid, walk
           around an' git in d' h'udder side.
Reverend: Well your husband must have to get out
           of bed too when you want to turn over.
Aunt: Oh no zir, no. Ee jus
           sheaves astern.

BIG STOMACHS COME COSTLY

Two years ago I was on holiday at the home of my in-laws in the Codroy Valley. While there a former resident of the Valley came to visit my mother in-law.

When I was introduced to her we had a pleasant conversation and then she said she had a story for me.

The story was that she had been married three times and was now a widow again. Her second husband had developed quite a large stomach. (a coroporation as we used to say.)

One afternoon they went to a lounge in the coumpany of a couple of their friends. The women had wine and the men had beer.

After an hour or so they got up to leave. On the way out through the lounge the men got about ten feet ahead of their wives.

As her husband passed one table, a client of the lounge looked up and was quite surprised to see a man with such a stomach as large as her husband's As she passed the table the man nudged his friend and pointed to her husband and said, "I wish I had what it cost to put dat pot on ee."

A TOUGH BUDGET

Uncle Joe was always asked his opinion on just about anything that the Municipal Council or the government was up to.

The budget for the city of Corner Brook had just been published that afternoon. Leaning over the fence that evening he was asked what in his opinion was the most interesting item in the budget. Well, he felt that the most interesting thing to him was the fact that the Humber River was only going to run twice a week.

LONG HAS TWO DIMENSIONS

An Island Cove man had a contract to build a house in St. John's. The necessary lumber was supposed to be on the site but after a few days he ran short of two by fours. He proceeded to Horwood Lumber Co. to obtain the extra stock. Being a good H'Island Cove feller he had to have some fun so when he was asked what he wanted he announced that he needed one hundred four by two's. The clerk corrected him and said he wanted two by four's. An argument broke out on the subject as follows:

MORE FROM BOB MACLEOD

Bob MacLeod entertained Newfoundlanders for fifty years. His piano and organ playing, his orchestra, radio and T.V. appearances, Gerald S. Doyle News Casting and his story telling is well remembered and will be for a long time to come.

The following is one of his stories and it actually happened.

Bob met an old acquaintenance from out of town. At the time this man had been married only 6 months and it was his second marriage. Bob asked him how was his new wife. "Well H'Uncle Bob sir, she's not 'alf nar quarter so good as me firse wife, but I'll get d'winter out of 'er".

He was organist and choir master at St. Andrews Presbyterian Church in St. John's for twenty-five years and your author was the Sunday School Superintendent for the same length of time. He said of Presbyterians—If 'it's fun, it's sinful.

Bob was one of the people whom I would meet and we did not have to say much to have a good laugh. He still enjoys a good yarn with his friends who visit him at the Glenbrook Lodge for Senior Citizens.

Like the famous Johnny Burke, Bob is capable of producing a ballad on the topic of the day or send you his thanks in verse as he did to me last Easter. On the following two pages is a sample. Sally's Cove electoral count produced a Newfoundland National predicament and Bob did it justice.

Dear Al, I takes me pen in hand to thank you for your gift so grand, We both enjoyed your cherry cake and ate it all left nar'a flake. In fact, me son, 'twas quite a dilly. And then, there came your Easter Lilly With Flowers just about to Burst. It looks so nice, 'Tis Number First". And for your Damson JAM—We send our thanks to you, our longtime Friend. Come in again, and have a "JAW". Till then "Long may your big jib draw."

THAT NIGHT IN SALLY'S COVE

You may talk of the election
of October twenty-eight
The P. C.'s and the Liberals
they each had quite a slate
And when it was all over
and the counting was all done
There was n'ar a soul in Newfoundland
could tell for sure who'd won.

The score was twenty-twenty
That's the way it all turned out
In Labrador Tom made it
But St. Barbe was still in doubt
Like Me and Ned—Trev said to Ed—
Though o'er the world we rove
We always will remember
That night in Sally's Cove.

Now soon before Judge Puddester
a recount did take place
To see for sure if Trev or Ed
had really won the race
But when they couldn't find the votes
said Justice Hal-by Jove!
I always will remember
that night in Sally's Cove.

Said Premier Joe—some years ago
go out and burn your boats
The people out in Sally's Cove
thought he said "Burn your votes"
So after the election
in Mrs. Payne's home
The ballots all went up in smoke
like in the Vatican in Rome.

Now to conclude and finish up
the truth I'll tell to you
We'll have to have another one
in Nineteen Seventy-two
'Cause Frank and Joe are like the man
who was hung up on the stove
The stove they burnt the ballots in
that night in Sally's Cove.

Bob MacLeod

HOW MUCH IS NONE

In June 1978 I was asked to come to Burgeo to address the graduating class. I lodged at the boarding house of Mr. & Mrs. Phillip Matthews. It was a delightful place to stay, they made you feel "right to home" welcome.

In any outport, which depends on the coastal boat for mail, it's normal that within an hour or so many people pay a visit to the post office to enquire if there is any mail for them.

This young fellow left the house, made a visit to the post office and came back and made this announcement, "I got d'mail. Dere was none".

CENSUS TAKING

A census taker was being frustrated by answers given by one older female individual whose replies were rather misleading. When it came to the matter of age she refused absolutely to answer. He proceeded diplomatically with other questions and returned to the subject of age.

Eventually she said, "Did you get the ages of the Misses Foster next door?"

Census taker: "Yes, I did. *Approximately* that is".

Lady: "Well my age is about the same as theirs".

By chance she got to look at the information on the Misses Foster. Under age she read, "AS OLD AS THE HILLS."

TAR AND BEER DON'T MIX

Two men from the Southern Shore always did things together. They fished and hunted jtogether and did odd jobs together.

On one occassion they had a job to come to St. John's and tar a roof. When they arrived at the house they discovered that the ladder they had was not long enough to reach the roof. It was necessary for them to go down town to get a longer one. Before they left they put the five gallon tin of tar on the woman's kitchen stove.

When passing the Belmont Tavern they could not resist going in for a few beers. Two hours later they remembered they had a job to do. They left the tavern and made for the street where they had to tar the roof, not bothering to look for a taller ladder.

One of the fellows stuttered and when he arrived at the street and turned into the street they stopped in their tracks and he remarked excitedly "Der-Der-Dere's, no-no trou-tou-touble to-to ga-get on the ro-ro-roof now, d'fi-fi-firemen's la-la-ladders are up dere".

THE MOONSHINE CAN

The following incident which took place several years after Confederation is true, but I am unable to relate the story using names and places. A young professional man was involved and he told me what happened. It has to do with the R.C.M.P., moonshine and bootlegging.

The professional man involved along with a couple of other men, would from time to time, get aboard their motor boat and travel to a certain community twenty miles distant. There they would pick up a cheap supply of moonshine, enough for themselves and an extra supply to sell.

On one particular trip they arrived at their supplier's house just as he was running off a batch of moonshine. He did not mind their seeing the operation because he had been selling these fellows shine for four or five years and he trusted them.

However, right in the middle of the run-off other people made a visit also, two R.C.M.P. officers. The officers had tried to catch the shiner on a few other occassions but were unsuccessful. This time there was no doubt, they had him red-handed.

But my friend was caught also. He told me he was never as unhappy in his life as when he was caught in this situation. He could visualize his being called as a material witness and also being charged himself for being on the premises for the purpose of purchasing moonshine, which was illegal. He said he just sat there in a cold sweat, not being allowed to leave, and imagined all the embarrassment this would cause him and his family. Since his employment was a position of public trust, he could see his job going out the window. To say the least, things looked very serious.

Well the R.C.M.P. took all the names and addresses of those on the premises; they also took over and disconnected all the

74

evidence, collected it all together and placed it on the bridge veranda) at the back door. They next held a small private conference, on the side to themselves. Then they presented the owner with a summons.

What took place next was rather a mild confrontation between one of the officers and the shiner. My friend told me that at the time what was said did not seem funny, and there was no rumour to this episode, but several hours later when the officers had left, it was food for a great laugh. He continued and said that the shiner was barking at the R.C.M.P. officer rather than talking civil like. You will see what I mean. The action went something like this. The officer presented the mooshine maker with a paper and said he was under arrest.

Shiner: WHAT ARREST?
Officer: For making moonshine.
Shiner: WHAT MOONSHINE?
Officer: The stuff we caught you making tonight.
Shiner: WHAT STUFF? WHAT NIGHT?
Officer: We have all the evidence
Shiner: WHAT EVIDENCE?
Officer: The Can
Shiner: WHAT CAN?
Officer: Well, all the equipment and things.
Shiner: WHAT THINGS?
Officer: They are out on your back bridge.
Shiner: WHAT BRIDGE?

At this point the officer motioned to the moonshine maker to follow him. They both went out the kitchen door onto the bridge. As in Ripley, believe it or not, the only item on the bridge was a lone rocking chair that had been there for many reasons. All the moonshine making equipment had disappeared. The whole "Sheebang", as we say in Newfoundland, had vanished into thin air. All of it had been removed by outside accomplices which no doubt were his children, which makes it an inside job rather than an outside one.

The officers searched for a couple of hours but no moonshine or equipment could they find.

After the officers had left the other visitors were given a tour which explained the evasion tactics and the clever hideout that had been used.

My friend laughed heartily as he told this story but said you can be sure he would never have a closer call than that one.

I have every respect for the R.C.M.P. and this story is being told without any suggestion of ridicule. I imagine the officers involved told the story themselves after sufficient time had elapsed.

MAKING SURE

Ye Olde Brigus Tea Rooms was the place to eat when making a motor trip around Conception Bay.

I am speaking of the days before Confederation and that means the days before we had the Trans Canada Highway. The Conception Bay Highway was the only road that was paved and naturally many people used it by choice, when out for a cruze.

The tea rooms at Brigus operated by Mrs. Peet and her sister, was the nicest place to eat and summertime their services were in great deman. Mrs. Peet also catered to weddings and banquets.

At one wedding reception, a bread roll had been placed on each side plate. While waiting to receive the cold turkey plate, for which Ye Olde Rooms were famous, a number of guests got up from their places and mingled amongst the other guests. Each one, on his return to his place, found that some one had eaten his bread roll.

One lady saw what was happening and when she got up to go to the washroom, she said, "Nobody is eatin' my roll". So she licked the roll all over and then proceeded to the washroom.

I could name the lady but I think I'd better not, she is friendly and humourous individual.

PRESCRIPTION FOR NOTHING

Dr. Walter Templeman was born in Bonavista but spent many years in Bell Island. He was dedicated to serving the people and was loved and revered by them.

Dr. Templeman was factual and had a good sense of humour. He had a few female patients who had imaginary problems and this at times got on Temp's nerves.

Mr. Lew Lawton was the druggist in Bell Island and he told the following story.

HIS APPLE JUICE SPECIMEN

Some years ago a gentleman from one of our outports, whom I could name, was in St. Clare's Mercy Hospital, St. John's, suffering from a kidney ailment. It was necessary for him to have urine specimens taken during the day but especially before and after meals.

He was a michevious type and one morning he thought he would have some fun. He knew the sister would be around to collect the specimen so this is what he did. He knew the specimen jar was clean but he made sure and washed it to his own satisfaction. He then poured the apple juice on his tray into it and waited.

The sister appeared soon afterwards and picking up the specimen jar remarked, "My it's a bit cloudy this morning". Our male patient took the jar from her hand saying, "Yes by gosh it is. Let's run it through again". With that, and to the amazement of the sister he downed the contents of the specimen jar.

DOGS CAN'T TAKE IT, BUT DOCTORS CAN

Dr. Walter Templeman spent many years serving the residents of Belt Island, Conception Bay. Sometimes people would call at night and he could tell pretty well whether they really needed a doctor or not. But he would always make sure and he would make the call.

Once when he had been out all evening making calls in a raging snow storm, he received one of these calls from a client who lived about two miles away. He felt it was one of those unnecessary calls. The husband assured him that his wife was truly sick this time. He consented but he told the man to come to meet him. "What?" the man said, "tackle up the horse and go out on a night like this. Doc, b'y, you wouldn't put a dog out on a night like this."

PLEASANT PUNISHMENT?

Many humourous incidents have taken place at the Salvation Army barracks in various communities and some Salvation Army officers have told me about them. I was visiting Burgeo and while there a travelling salesman told me about his youthful days on Pilley's Island. He often went to the barracks on Sunday nights.

He remembered one person who testified each meeting night without fail. It was Aunt Suse and she always told about her week's doings, good or bad.

On one occassion she was not very proud of her actions for the past week and testified to the fact. She told how h'ugly she'd been with 'er 'usband Garge and all the chillun. She finished on a repentive note and catching sight of the big wood box by the wall she said. "My, my, I feels so 'shamed dat I feels I should be hidin' down be'ind d'woodbox dere".

Very few minutes passed when Uncle Jabez got to his feet to make his testimony. He was in the same mood and tone as Aunt Suse and he finished by saying, "I feels just so 'shamed as Aunt Suse, an I t'inks I should be down be'ind d'wood box 'long wid'er".

LAUGHTER AND RELIGION

The Bible says, "Every good gift comes from God". I believe laughter is a gift of God.

Reading and studying recently from a book titled "How to Pray", I noticed there was a prayer. "For a Sense of Humour". This prayer started as follows, "Our Father in Heaven, how patient you are with us, your children, who constantly break life's traffic rules; how wonderful is your sense of humour, making heaven tingle with your laughter at the silly things men do".

We must remember that Jesus lived here on earth and no doubt in his time there were many things to laugh at in daily life, just as there is today. Surely he laughed along with all the people with whom he mixed. No religion should portray a solemn and gloomy look. Living a good Christian life should make us happy, and laughter is one of the ingredients of happiness.

I have heard of many humourous things that happened in the chapel or outside it which have been the result of things done or said at Church meetings. There is room for laughter in Church.

The Reverend D. D. Oswald Hoffman, Spiritual leader of the Lutheran Church of America was in Newfoundland for the Bible Society in 1979.

During his address one evening he said, "The Lord and twelve men travelling around the country side had to have lots of laughs. For instance when James and John invited the Lord as follows, "Lord, call down fire from heaven and consume these hecklers". Jesus only response to their suggestion was to call the brothers, "Sons of Thunder".

A member of the Salvation Army told me of a funny incident in Corner Brook. The major's father-in-law had come to visit and he also was a Salvation Army man.

He got up and testified but he had some difficulty deciding when he was finished. On several occassions the man would be almost sitting on his chair when he would suddenly straighten up and continue with his testimony for another couple of minutes. This happened three or four times and he eventually finished and sat down.

As soon as he did sit down a woman got to her feet and said loud enough for everyone to hear, "I knows 'tis nice for the major's father-in-law to visit but 'tis not very often we haves a man who doesn't know when he wants to sit down".

A DOLLAR

A certain R.C. priest never failed to mention money either in his sermon or when the week's schedule was being announced.

On one occassion a Mass was being held for one of his deceased parishoners. He delivered the euology and then spoke on another aspect of life by saying,

TORONTO

NEWFOUNDLAND'S *BIGGEST OUTPORT*

BROTHER

In evangelestic denominations everyone is referred to as brother and sister. Capt. Snook, of the Salvation Army, told me about a sad, yet humourous incident which he experienced on new Gower Street.

He stopped by a very drunk man who was lying on the side-walk, "dead to the world" as we say. He was very much sound asleep. From his general appearance he had been in a fight. His face was dirty and unshaven and there were several bruises. His suit was also very dirty and torn in a number of places. He was a specimen of humanity at that time, whom nobody would care to claim as a near relative.

However, a citizen came along just as Capt. Snook was about to lift the drunk and have him transported to a safer place to rest. The citizen said, "WHO'S THAT"? Capt. Snook turned to him and exclaimed emphatically, "THAT'S YOUR BROTHER"!

Mr. Citizen moved away quickly not believing his ears.

OVERHEARD

An old lady was reading from the newspaper. It was about something a person had done that shocked the community. She put the paper down and said "Well, it takes all kinds to make a world, but I'm glad I'm not one of them".

A RED LIGHT MEANS?

A nurse in St. John's was hurrying to be on duty by the prescribed time of 4:00 P.M. She was driving faster than usual and had beaten two red lights. The third light proved her downfall. The light was yellow alright but went red just as she entered the intersection.

It took only a few seconds and when she looked in the mirror, yes sir, there he was right on her bumper with his revolving red light flashing. She pulled to the curb and it was not long before he was asking for her license.

She produced the licence as he said, Policeman: Do you know what a red light means? Nurse: Yes! Someone wants the bed pan.

UNCLE JOHN HAD LIGHT AFTER DEATH

The Lions Club of Bloomfield-Musgravetown had a birthday party at which I was invited to speak.

Before I left Bloomfield a gentleman related the following story.

He explained that when the various communities around Newfoundland were being electrified, not every one could afford to have their house wired. A common thing for them to say was, "they couldn't afford to get the lights in."

An old man died down in Bunion's Cove and two men were engaged to dig the grave. Before they finished their digging it became dark. They arranged with a man living near the graveyard and close to the grave site, to bring a wire from his house so they could keep digging and finish the job before they went home. Another old gentleman saw the light down in the graveyard and said to himself,

R. C.'S ARE WORSE THAN PROTESTANTS

A story has been told of Reverend Father Coady when thieves had gotten into his car.

Amongst other things which Father had purchased that day were two bottles of rum. When he arrived home to Tor's Cove, he discovered that one bottle was missing.

He remarked, "Now, what do you think of that Protestant that stole that bottle of rum?" And his visitor asked, "Why do you think it was a Protestant, Father?" Father Coady replied, "Cuz if it was an R.C. he would have taken both of them."

SAUSAGES

In Magistrates court in St. John's, years ago, a man was before court for making sausages using tainted meat.

Considerable evidence was taken. An employee of the accused was in the witness box. The judge asked quite a few questions and received a number of evasive answers.

Then the Judge asked him, "Well, would you say the meat was good for human consumption?" The reply, "No yer honour, but t'was good for sausages dough".

RETALLIATION ENOUGH

Two brothers who lived in Bell Island had spent most of their lives fishing together and from the same boat.

On one occassion Bill made a gross error while on the fishing grounds and Joe gave him what for verbally. He called him many things and bawled him out royally.

ST. PETER OR ST. PATRICK

The Mother Superior had warned that no one who came to the convent looking for help should be turned away empty handed.

One day the door bell rang and a young novice went to the door. She was only there about half a minute when the door shut. The Mother Superior was coming down the stairway and enquired who was at the door. Yes, it was some one looking for food and the Mother said, "Oh my my, and you turned him away. Do you know you may have turned away St. Peter?" The young novice replied, "By the smell on his breath. Mother, it could have been St. Patrick".

HARD TO PLEASE

A couple of co-workers were coming off shift and one said, "Come on, let's go and have a beer". His friend replied, "No b'y, I got to go home and explain". "Explain What?" "I don't know. I have to wait until I go home".

The same fellow had a wife who was difficult to please and it did not matter what he did he should have done it the other way.

When his birthday came around she went shopping and bought him two ties. When he was dressing he saw the package and opened it. He thought he might please his wife by wearing one of the ties right away that morning. When he came to breakfast she looked across the table at him and remarked, "Ah! You didn't like the other one, did ya".

PRECISE INSTRUCTIONS

While at Halifax in November 1979, I visited the office of my book distributor, H. H. Marshall Ltd. While there I met a gentleman who had been to St. John's for his first time in 1975.

While there, Mr. Herb Pike invited him to visit on Sunday at his brother's residence in Barneed, Conception Bay. He would have to drive to Barneed on his own and explicit instructions were given to him regarding the turn off point from Conception Bay. The turn off point was Hibb's Hole.

When he arrived at this turn off point he wished to be certain so he stopped the car to confirm the next leg of his journey. An older gentleman was standing near the turn off and the following conversation took place:

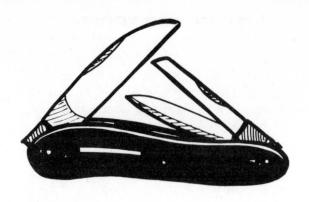

THE PASSABLE FAIR COOK

Since my book, "Come 'Ere Till I Tells Ya", was published in 1978 I have received many letters telling me how much the factual folklore humour of Newfoundland was enjoyed. Many said how the humour gave the laughs we all need. One lady in British Columbia thanked me for the "clean" reading.

One letter I received describes the type of Newfoundlander that I try to portray to my readers. This letter describes the versatile self sufficient Newfoundlander who can turn his hand to most anything. Also he has the sense of humour told in this book.

He's not from Sin Jan's he's from "over 'ome."

Dear Al,

Just finished reading "Come 'Ere Till I Tell Ya". Good stuff! Thought you might be interested in hearing a couple of yarns about a Newfoundlander with whom I was shipmates some years ago. His first name was Alex and his last name doesn't matter. Suffice it to say that he possessed the average Newfoundlander's happy facility for being able to turn his hand to any practical task. He was a very good deckhand, a passable fair cook, he could cut your hair and could have worked porfessionally as a tailor.

The task of a ship's cook is a demanding one. It is a 7-day a week vocation; days start early and run late and there is little time for the cook to spend ashore when the vessel is in port. In my opinion he is, next to the master, the most important man on the ship. If the food is good, seamen will endure a surprising amount of inconvenience with little or no grumbling, but let the quality of the food drop and trouble soon breaks out.

Once we were short a cook and Alex had turned to the galley

hores, and found that it was cutting into his shore leave rather
nore than he wished. One morning he appeared at the mate's
abin and said, "Mr. Mate, I'd like to have the afternoon off. My
ister's dead". The mate, a rather old and kindly man, was
roperly sympathetic. He urged Alex to take 2 or 3 days if he
eeded it, and we would somehow manage to shift for ourselves
s far as meals were concerned. Alex, however, to the mate's
urprise, was back in the galley next morning. The mate thought
 odd that Alex could have concluded matters concerning his
ister so quickly. In the course of the conversation he asked, "By
ie way, when did your sister die?" Alex looked straight at him
nd with a perfectly straight face replied, "Forty-five years ago,
ir!"

On another occasion we were tied up in a port where strict
ecurity measures were maintained. It was necessary to pass
hrough a security check point at the head of the dock before
ntering the city. The guards interpreted the word "Security"
uite literally, and searched every package passing through,
owever small. One evening Alex appeared at the gate carrying a
mall satchel, which the guard immediately demanded to inspect.
Oh no!", said Alex, "I've got a cat in here! A chap gave it to
ie." He insisted on opening the satchel, despite Alex's protest
hat the cat would get away. He slid back the zipper, and sure
nough, a large healthy cat popped out and streaked away at top
peed. "Dammit!", said Alex, "Now it's going to take half the
ight to catch him again!" So saying he took off, presumably in
ursuit of the cat. Some hour and a half later he again appeared
t the gate. "I got him!" he announced triumphantly, patting the
atchel, and the guard waved him through carrying his four
uarts of contraband liquor!

Yours truly,

THE GENERAL STORE KEEPERS

(All names had to be omitted)

Here is a story about a storekeeper and his wife who made very good business partners. Neither one of them had a lot of education. The wife was the one with the arithmetic and naturally she looked after the books. His particular ability was that he served shop all day, and at night would remember all charged goods and tell his wife just what each customer had charged to his or her account.

There was one evening, however, that he was rather puzzled. He knew that one of their clients had bought a sou-wester rain hat, but which client it was he could not remember. They solved the problem by charging all sixty-one clients with the hat but they charged it in this fashion—

One sou-wester—$3.00 (or we think you had it).

This was done expecting all those who did not have the sou-wester would say so. But no one did. So they got paid for 61 hats instead of one.

When someone died in the settlement it was quite customary for all the ladies to wear black stockings at the funeral. On one occassion the stock of black stockings ran out very quickly. Rachel said not to worry she would have a new stock by morning. That night she took most of her stock of white stockings and dyed them black. No problem, next day there were plenty of black stockings to satisfy the demand.

When a new shipment of boots or shoes arrived, the laces were removed from the boxes.

If a customer for boots or shoes came in, it was normal for the prospective purchaser to ask for a better price. No, no there could be no better price on the boots or shoes.

When this situation occurred it was usual for a little hagling to go on until Rachel would consult with Joe and the result was always the same. "No we can't make a better price, but what we will do is to throw in the laces for the one price".

Sale consumated.

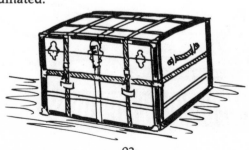

YOU PAY EXTRA FOR WORMS

A couple of months ago I was talking with a man from Fogo Island, who is now living in St. John's.

He told me about a purchase of a couple of pounds of fresh cod fish which had worms in it. Two weeks later he made another purchase of fish from a different fish store. As he was about to leave the store he casually said to the proprietor, "I suppose there are no worms in this fish?" To which the proprietor replied, "WORMS, YOU'RE LUCKY TO GET THE FISH AT THAT PRICE!"

NEWFOUNDLANDERS GET HOMESICK

When the Second World War broke out the face of many areas of Newfoundland changed considerably. One area was the farm land to the east of St. John's. What was known as Ross's Farm and Woodley's Farm was the land which the United Stated purchased to build a head quarters and training camp for their operations in Newfoundland, now known as Fort Pepperall. Argentia became a U.S. Naval Base and at Stephenville the U.S. built an air force base.

This all came about through an agreement between Churchill and Roosevelt. England needed war ships. The United States had war ships in mothballs. The deal was made that the United States would get bases in Newfoundland and in return the U.S. would supply fifty destroyers to England.

Although, unfortunately, it took a war to do it, Newfoundland enjoyed a tremendous economic boom.

All this construction gave Newfoundland's carpenters, plumbers and electricians uninterrupted job opportunities during the war and for about ten years afterwards.

Most of the carpenters were men from the outports.

Now there is a tradition in Newfoundland which has not entirely disappeared. Men who would leave home in the spring to work in other parts of Newfoundland or on construction jobs in the U.S.A., mostly in the Boston area, in the fall would "down tools" and set out for home. It was a well known and accepted practice that Newfoundlanders went home in the fall. There were good reasons for this. There was work at home. Things had to be "put to rights" for the coming winter. And during the winter the men had to go into the woods to cut firewood, because Newfoundland for centuries depended on wood for fuel. A point of interest is that wood cut this winter would be the wood used next year or even two years hence. The wood was green when cut and had to dry to be of practical use for fuel. A year's supply had to be cut ahead.

During the war boom in Newfoundland, American foremen were appauled that a man would leave a good job, just to be at home for four or five months. These foremen did not know that Newfoundlanders "went home in the fall."

An Irishman, an American and a Newfoundlander all arrived at the gate of heaven at the same time. St. Peter addressed the

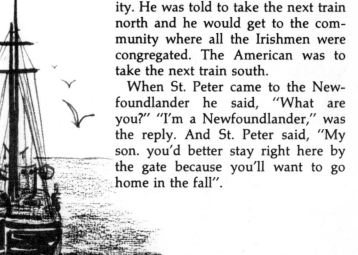

Irishman first and asked his nationality. He was told to take the next train north and he would get to the community where all the Irishmen were congregated. The American was to take the next train south.

When St. Peter came to the Newfoundlander he said, "What are you?" "I'm a Newfoundlander," was the reply. And St. Peter said, "My son. you'd better stay right here by the gate because you'll want to go home in the fall".

GUNS ARE ONLY STICKS!

During the early days of the Second World War, the United States of America was granted three areas in Newfoundland as military bases.

They were Fort Pepperrell at Pleasantville near St. John's, Harmon Air Force Base at Stephenville, and the Marine Naval Base at Argentia.

May I say that was in 1940 and the authorities in Ottawa were not too happy about having military bases, belonging to any nation, so close to the shores of Canada. They complained to Britan and Churchill said not to be so concerned you will have Newfoundland after the war. Ask yourself what happened?

However, as well as having naval facilities at Argentia, the Americans had an air base. It was agreed that when weather conditions proved it necessary, some civilian air craft would be allowed to land there.

At the Argentia Naval Base very tight security existed. Every civilian landing at Argentia was considered an alien visitor. Guards stood at the gangway and each passenger from the Air Canada aircraft was watched closely.

On one occcossion Air Canada was carrying almost a full load of young Newfoundlanders who had been to Western Canada to aid in farm work, and were now returning home. Two American naval personnel stood on each side of the gangway. For some reason the line of passengers stopped and one young Newfoundland farm hand found a fixed bayonet touching his belly. He looked down to see what it was and when he saw the bayonet he said, "Look 'ere butty, if you don't take dat stick out of me guts, I'LL RAM IT DOWN YER T'ROAT."

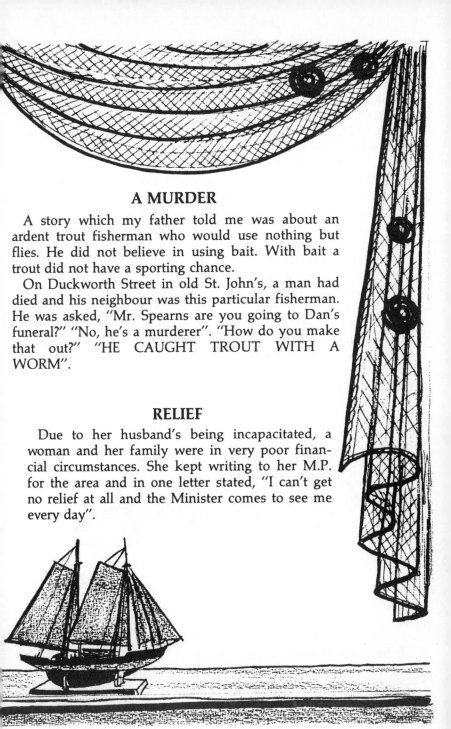

A MURDER

A story which my father told me was about an ardent trout fisherman who would use nothing but flies. He did not believe in using bait. With bait a trout did not have a sporting chance.

On Duckworth Street in old St. John's, a man had died and his neighbour was this particular fisherman. He was asked, "Mr. Spearns are you going to Dan's funeral?" "No, he's a murderer". "How do you make that out?" "HE CAUGHT TROUT WITH A WORM".

RELIEF

Due to her husband's being incapacitated, a woman and her family were in very poor financial circumstances. She kept writing to her M.P. for the area and in one letter stated, "I can't get no relief at all and the Minister comes to see me every day".

WOULD YOU BELIEVE IT?

Visiting with some friends one evening I was happy to find myself in the company of a married couple from Notre Dame Bay. I found their company very pleasant and entertaining.

The wife told some humourous stories from their lives, things that actually happened. The one I found most humourous was from their courting days.

The story is that in their courting days they lived in Notre Dame Bay but in two outports six miles apart. Transportation was such that Jack had to walk the six miles four times a week to see his intended Flossie. On his way he always dropped in to see his friend Mickey, who lived very close to Jack's own house.

On one particular evening Jack made his visit to Mickey's and after a short stay proceeded on his way as usual. He was gone about an hour and a half when he appeared again at Mickey's. Mickey looked at Jack rather surprised saying, "What's happend Jack, you were here once before this evening"? Suddenly Jack appeared to come to his senses and exclaimed "OH MY GOSH! I turned around to put me back to the wind to light me pipe and forgot to turn around again".

His wife confirmed the story saying, "That was one night I wasn't very much on his mind".

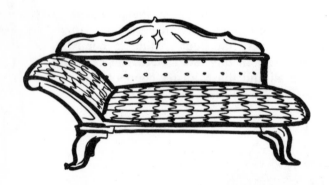

WHERE ARE THOSE PLACES?

It had been a great night of laughter, and it makes things go well if people can laugh without effort. On this occassion a lady came up to me and paid me the most unusual compliment by saying, "My H'Uncle Al, I've a laughed in places tonight I've never laughed before."

AUCTION 120 AND THE HIGH REQUIEM MASS

For anyone who plays Newfoundland's most famous card game called "Auction 120", the following should prove to be a top story.

Mr. Sol Fry, who worked with our company for nearly fifty years, and is now deceased, related the following to be.

The Elks Club on Duckworth Street is where Mr. Fry played a regular game of "Auction 120" with the same four people partaking. This continued for some years until the Elks Club moved to Carpasian Road which proved to be rather a chore for Mr. Fry to get to this location. The result was that these games of auction, of the same four, came to an end.

Some years later, Joe, a member of the four died. Mr. Fry saw the death notice in the Evening Telegram and decided to attend Joe's funeral service at the Bascilica. The High Requiem Mass was said for Joe, and Mr. Fry gave considerable significance to this fact although he had never himself heard this Mass before.

Seeing some people he knew at the grave side, he got rather close to them and made the following statement, "Anyone who goes thirty for sixty on the Queen *and makes it,* deserves the High Requiem Mass". One of the mourners could not help laughing very silently within and shook until she was sitting on the concrete around the grave.

The story behind this is that Joe on one occasion went thirty for sixty on the Queen of Spades and made it. His partners had the five high trumps above the Queen, the King, Ace, Ace of Hearts, Jack and Five.

Yes, I agree with Mr. Fry. Who wouldn't?

UNIVERSITY
A TRUE STORY FROM THE MEMORIAL UNIVERSITY OF NEWFOUNDLAND

A professor of Religious Studies at the University verified this story because he was the lecturer who experienced it and told me how it happened.

One of the courses on religion at the University introduces the student very quickly to three major religions: Judaism, Christianity and Islam. During the brief survey of the three religions all that can be done is to highlight the main beliefs of each. The major emphasis is placed on what the best representatives of each of these religions believe about God.

One day, at the end of the course when the lecturer was answering any last minute questions prior to a test, one student said: "Sir, if I was one of ye, I'd believe nutting at all."

The lecturer, taken aback a bit, asked him, "Why would you say a thing like that?"

"Well sir," he said, "where I comes from there is only one religion, and until I came in here I taught it was d'only religion. Now I knows it isn't d'only religion, and it may not be d'roight religion, and for the rest I'm roight confused."

"In that case," replied the lecturer, "I think we should take time to talk about this confusion. I don't want anyone either to be confused or upset. What bothers you particularly?"

"Well," he said, "when we talked about de Jews you said some wonderful t'ings about dem. I can't find a t'ing wrang with what dey believes. If what you said is true."

"Yes," replied the teacher, "all I told you was d'truth."

"Now den, you said some good tings about d'Muslims, and what dey believes about God and all. And if dey believes about God what you said, den I can't find much wrang with dem eider. If all you said was d'truth."

"Yes," replied the lecturer, "all I told you was the truth."

"Now den," said the young fellow, "if dey Jews is all roight, and I thinks dey is, and if the Muslims ain't wrong, and I tinks dey are roight too, and if the Catalic Church ain't d'only church and ain't necessarily the roight church, what are we goin' to say about de Pentecosts?"

(After the suspense that had built up in the class as a result of not knowing what he might say next, the class broke up into an uproar of laughter,—not the least of those who enjoyed it were the Pentecostals themselves.)

THE GRAVE DIGGER

To be sure, the Irish have a homour all of their own.

I was invited to come to Catalina to a Senior Citizen's party. While I was there a man related a story about a resident of Melrose, three miles away, who had died last fall. The relatives had made a request of a young fellow who was a neighbor. The request was that he go to the graveyard and assist in the digging of the grave for the deceased Patrick.

His answer was "No! Patrick could have had it done. He was walkin' around here all summer doin' nothin'".

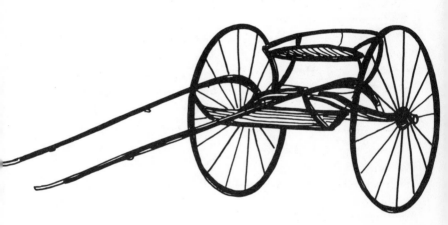

IT MADE NO DIFFERENCE

A very good friend of mine, a professor at the Memorial University, told me about a new professor who came to the University in September, 1978.

Anne Marie was in his own classes for two years. She was one girl who never failed to express herself without making very clear what she meant.

When our new professor was only there ten days he stopped when he was halfway through his lecture and said, "Am I going too fast?" Anne Marie spoke up and replied, "Don't worry about it prof. 'Tis not worth slowin' up for".

GLOSSARY

Annuder	Another	Lun	Side—Protected from the wind
'arn	Horn		
Arse	Horse	Mawning	Morning
Agin	Against	Mose	Most
Bid	Bed	Mout	Mouth
Breeze	Push	Nar	None or Neither
Cartny	Certainly	Neider	Neither
Cuddy	Bow	Oi	I
Carr	Carry	Over 'ome	At home in the outports
Cruze	Cruise		
Chile Birt	Child Birth	Put to rights	Put in order—Get ready
Dough	Though		
Down Tools	Stop Work	Salt Junk	Corned Beef
Ee	He	Shinying	Playing a scratch game of hockey
Eh	He		
'ead	Head	Settle	Couch
En	Him	Slouse	Splash
Een	In	Sheebang	All of it—The works
Feesh	Fish		
Feesh & Brews	Newfoundland's National Dish	Sauve	Save
		Taut	Thought
Fauder	Father	Toime	Time, meaning a party
Firse	First		
Firse Rate	Pretty Good	Udder	Other
Galilay	Galilee	Vulled	Filled
Hauled Off	Laying Off	Waz	Was
Hudder	Other	Wuz	Was
In 'arder	In order—get ready for	Wunaful	Wonderful
		Windy	Window
Jus	Just	Yistidy	Yesterday
		Youse	You

Ryans And The Pittmans

We'll rant and we'll roar — like true New-found-lan-ders We'll rant and we'll roar on deck and be-low Un-till we see bot-tom in-side the two sunk-ers When straight through the chan-nel to Tos-low we'll go.

I'm a son of a sea-cook, and a cook in a trader;
I can dance, I can sing, I can reef the main-boom,
I can handle a jigger, and cuts a big figure
Whenever I gets in a boat's standing room.

If the voyage is good, then this fall I will do it;
I wants two pound ten for a ring and the priest,
A couple o' dollars for clane shirt and collars,
And a handful o' coppers to make up a feast.

There's plump little Polly, her name is Goldsworthy;
There's John Coady's Kitty, and Mary Tibbo;
There's Clara from Bruley, and young Martha Foley,
But the nicest of all is my girl in Toslow.

Farewell and adieu to ye fair ones of Valen,
Farewell and adieu to ye girls in the Cove;
I'm bound to the Westward, to the wall with the hole in,
I'll take her from Toslow the wild world to rove.

Farewell and adieu to ye girls of St. Kyran's,
Of Paradise and Presque, Big and Little Bona,

I'm bound unto Toslow to marry sweet Biddy,
And if I don't do so, I'm afraid of her da.

I've bought me a house from Katherine Davis,
A twenty-pound bed from Jimmy McGrath;
I'll get me a settle, a pot and a kettle;
Then I'll be ready for Biddy—Hurrah!

I brought in the Ino this spring from the city
Some rings and gold brooches for the girls in the Bay;
I bought me a case-pipe—they call it a meerschaum—
It melted like butter upon a hot day.

I went to a dance one night at Fox Harbour;
There were plenty of girls, so nice as you'd wish,
There was one pretty maiden a-chawing of frankgum,
Just like a young kitten a-gnawing fresh fish.

Then here is a health to the girls of Fox Harbour,
Of Oderin and Presque, Crabbes Hole and Bruley.
Now let ye be jolly, don't be melancholy.
I can't marry all, or in chokey I'd be.

Words by H. W. LeMessurier, C.M.G.

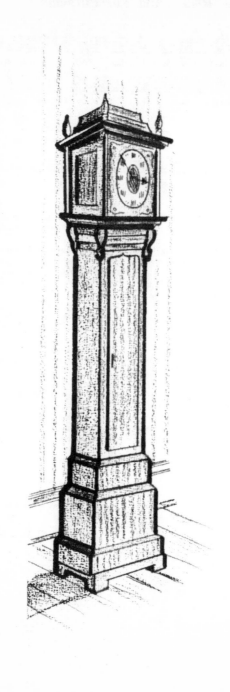